Real Estate Investing

And Credit Repair Strategies

Make a Killer Profit By Taking an Unfair

Advantage Of These Credit Repair Secrets

And Real Estate Investment

Opportunities

By

Michael Ezeanaka

www.MichaelEzeanaka.com

Copyright ©2019

Disclaimer

This publication is designed to provide competent and reliable information regarding the subject matter covered. However, it is sold with the understanding that the author is not engaged in rendering investment or other professional advice. Laws and practices often vary from state to state and country to country and if investment or other expert assistance is required, the services of a professional should be sought. The author specifically disclaims any liability that is incurred from the use or application of the contents of this book.

Books In The Business and Money Series	
Series #	**Book Title**
1	Affiliate Marketing
2	Passive Income Ideas
3	Affiliate Marketing + Passive Income Ideas (2-in-1 Bundle)
4	Facebook Advertising
5	Dropshipping
6	Dropshipping + Facebook Advertising (2-in-1 Bundle)
7	Real Estate Investing For Beginners
8	Credit Cards and Credit Repair Secrets
9	Real Estate Investing And Credit Repair (2-in-1 Bundle)
10	Passive Income With Affiliate Marketing (2nd Edition)
The kindle edition will be available to you for FREE when you purchase the paperback version from Amazon.com (The US Store)	

This book is a **2-in-1 Bundle** Consisting of Books 7 and 8 in the table above.

Download The Audio Versions Along With The Complementary PDF Document For FREE from **www.MichaelEzeanaka.com/My Audiobooks**

Real Estate Business Scorecard

How would you like to download a scorecard that **neatly summarizes**, in a table each Real Estate Business Model's score across 5 areas – Liquidity, Scalability, Potential return on investment, Passivity and Simplicity? If you want it, a PDF version of the card is hosted on my **website** and can be downloaded for free. However, a password is required to unlock the download. Follow the steps below to **retrieve the password**!

Steps to take

1. The password consists of 8 characters (all lower case)
2. Here is the incomplete password: p-k-n-b-
3. The **second**, **fourth**, **sixth** and **eighth** character of the password is missing and is located in random pages of this book.
4. **Read this book** carefully to locate and retrieve them (they're so obvious you can't miss them).
5. Once you have the complete password then go to www.MichaelEzeanaka.com > Free Stuff > Ebooks/Audiobooks > Real Estate Business Scorecard, download the business scorecard and enjoy!

Table of Contents

Part 1 – Real Estate Investing For Beginners

Part 2 - Credit Card And Credit Repair Secrets

Part I

Real Estate Investing

For Beginners

Earn Passive Income

With Reits, Tax Lien Certificates, Lease,

Residential and Commercial Real Estate

By

Michael Ezeanaka

www.MichaelEzeanaka.com

Introduction

Real estate has long been one of the most popular assets to invest in. After all, land is something that people will always need to build their homes and businesses on. As an asset, real estate provides the potential for multiple income streams.

There are many ways through which you can benefit from investing in real estate. As a direct owner, you can refurbish a building and rent it out to a tenant to generate a fairly passive income or you can resell (flip) it. But you can also make money without actually owning property.

In most cases, property values appreciate over time. This means that you can sell it for a higher amount in the future or use it to raise capital that you can reinvest.

Real estate investments can provide you with passive income. There are ways that you can make money from real estate that don't require you to exert a lot of effort and time. You don't even need to directly own real estate in order for this to happen.

Moreover, your income from real estate investments is not affected by inflation. If anything, your rental income will increase along with inflation. This means that you will be able to enjoy a higher cash flow while maintaining or improving the purchasing power of your money.

There are tax benefits too. If you have investment property, you are allowed to deduct deprecation of the building and any additional capital investments, which will reduce your taxable income. And there are other tax advantages you can enjoy based on what investment method you use.

In this book, we will describe the various methods that you can use to invest in real estate. Like we said before, you don't actually need to be a direct owner of property in order to make money from it. We will give you an overview of each investment method, including the pros and cons of each one.

Each real estate investment method will be scored using this set of criteria:

- **Liquidity** – this refers to how easy it is to convert your investment into cash if you suddenly need the money.
- **Scalability** – this refers to how easy it is to increase your investment.
- **Potential Return on Investment** – this is how much income you can gain from the investment considering your costs and expenses.
- **Passivity** – this refers to how easy it will be to earn money without much time and effort.
- **Simplicity** – this refers to how easy it is to get started with an investment.

Most, if not all, of the *basic information* that you need to examine and evaluate your real estate investment options are in this book. There are also tips for success at the end of each chapter to guide you in your investment activities.

Without further ado, let's get right into it!

Interesting Fact #1

Most people don't realise it but McDonalds is not a burger flipping-restaurant chain; it is one of the worlds best real estate portfolios. Franchisees do the burger flipping and McDonalds gets paid handsomely for owning the best commercial real estate all over the world!

Congratulations!

The second character of the password required to unlock the *Real Estate Business Scorecard* is letter m.

Chapter 1

Real Estate Investment Trusts

Real Estate Investment Trusts (REITs) are companies that invest in commercial real estate properties, and allow investors to buy shares in them. They are designed to make investing in real estate **more accessible** by making the amount of money needed more affordable. For instance, a shopping mall costs millions of dollars to build, making investing in them prohibitive for most investors. However, by buying shares in an REIT that specializes in shopping malls, you can have exposure to this type of investment for a relatively small capital outlay.

A Short History of REITs

REITs were first created in 1960 via Public-Law 86-779 under President Dwight Eisenhower, as a way of making investment in large-scale real estate more accessible to the ordinary investor with limited funds. The first REIT to be established under the new law was the American Realty Trust in 1961.

Initially, REITs mostly invested in mortgage companies, which helped fuel the growth of the real estate industry in the sixties and seventies. The funds invested by the REITs were used to invest in construction and land development.

In 1992, Retail REIT Taubman Centers expanded the scope of REITs by creating the UPREIT. UPREITs allowed REITs to enter into an "operating partnership" with an existing partnership. Under this agreement, the partnership contributes properties that the REIT is the majority owner of. In exchange for the properties, the partners have the right to exchange these for cash or shares in the REIT.

At present, over 30 countries have their own REIT regimes. A global index to track both REITs and the global property market in general, the FTSE EPRA/ Nareit Global Real Estate Series, was created in 2001. According to this index, there were 477 real estate companies from 35 countries that listed in the stock exchange, accounting for a $2 trillion equity market capitalization, as of December 2017. REITs accounted for around 78% of the total capitalization.

Types of REITs

There are three general categories of REITs:

- Equity REITs are those that directly invest in real estate, either by financing their development or by purchasing already existing properties. The REIT generates income by renting out to tenants and distributes these to shareholders as dividends.

- Mortgage REITs, on the other hand, invest in real estate mortgages, either by lending money for real estate loans or by buying mortgage-backed securities. They generate income through the interest they earn from the loans, less the cost of funding the loans (net interest margin).

- Hybrid REITs. These are REITs that invest in real estate and mortgage loans. Hybrid REITs are generally in the minority, although they generally are weighted on one investment type over the other.

In order to qualify as a REIT, the company must be an entity that is taxable as a corporation and meet the following requirements:

- It must have at least 100 shareholders
- It must distribute at least 90% of its taxable income annually to shareholders
- No more than half of its shares should be held by five or less shareholders
- At least 75% of its gross income should come from rents, sales of real estate or interest on mortgages financing real estate
- It should be managed by a board of directors/trustees

Equity REITs

We are focusing our discussion on equity REITs, since these are the most-commonly invested in. Thus, whenever we refer to REITs, we are talking about equity REITs. Mortgage REITs will be referred to as mREITs.

The majority of equity REITs focus on a particular type of property, although there are some that have a diversified portfolio. The most common types of REITs are:

- **Retail** - These REITs invest in retail properties such as shopping malls and freestanding outlets. One example is Realty Income, whose portfolio focuses on freestanding, single-tenant properties that are rented out to warehouse clubs, drugstores and other retail businesses. Realty Income has 5,326 properties in its portfolio and its major tenants include 7-11, FedEx, Walgreens and AMC Theaters.

- **Healthcare** - These REITs invest in properties that are rented to tenants that provide health care services such as hospitals, skilled nursing facilities and elderly housing facilities. An example is Ventas, which has a diversified portfolio that consists of both real estate leased on a net-lease basis and run through operating partnerships with companies like Altria Senior Living.

- **Hotel** - These REITs invest in luxury hotels, budget motels or destination resorts. An example of a hotel REIT is Apple Hospitality, whose portfolio focuses on properties that are operated under the Marriott and Hilton brands.

- **Industrial** - These REITs are focused on factory and warehouse properties. An example is STAG Industrial, which specializes in single-tenant properties and has 360 properties in 37 states.

- **Residential** - These REITs focus mainly on apartments. One example is Avalon Bay Communities whose portfolio of apartment communities is mainly centered in leading metropolitan areas such as New York/New Jersey Metro, New England and the Pacific Northwest.

- **Data centers** - These REITs operate and own facilities that lease to companies that provide data protection and storage services. An example of a data center REIT is Equinx, which is the largest publicly traded REIT of this type, and operates close to 200 data centers in five continents.

It should be noted that the dividends you receive from REITs are called distributions. The reason for this is that distributions are treated differently than dividends for tax purposes. REIT distributions are divided into three categories:

- **Dividends**. These are taxed as ordinary income, up to a maximum 39.6% rate plus a 3.8% investment income surcharge.
- **Return of capital.** This portion is nontaxable in the year you received it and will also reduce your taxable income. However, you will have to pay tax on it when you sell your shares. They will be taxed as either long-term or short-term capital gains, based on how long you held on to the shares.
- **Capital gains.** If you receive this as part of your disbursement, you will be taxed at the short-term or long-term capital gains rate during the year you received it.

The REIT will make it easy to declare your distributions on your taxes by sending you IRS Form 1099-DIV, which breaks them down for you.

Mortgage REITs

Mortgage REITs are an alternative to equity REITs that provide higher yields, but also require you to accept higher risks. MREITs actually make up only a small percentage of total traded REITs but they are popular among investors who are willing to accept the risks they entail in exchange for the high dividends they generate. As of 2017, there are 222 REITs listed, of which 181 are equity REITs and 41 are mortgage REITs.

Instead of buying real estate, mREITs purchase mortgages and mortgage-backed securities. By doing so, they provide mortgage credit for individual homebuyers as well as businesses that want to invest in commercial real estate.

To raise capital, however, they rely on equity and leverage. They can raise equity by making secondary stock offerings. Using leverage, however, can be a double-edged sword. Using high amounts of debt allows the mREIT to increase its holdings and the potential profits it can earn. However, if market conditions are unfavorable, higher leverage can increase potential losses since the cost of paying loans will be more than what it earns from its holdings.

MREITs are vulnerable to changes in both long-term and short-term interest rates, and thus you have to be prepared for the volatility they cause in order to remain profitable. If interest rates fall, more homeowners may pre-pay their loans, reducing the amount of income the mREIT generates. But if interest rates rise, the mREIT's holdings may lose their value, and its share prices may fall.

Non-Traded REITs

These are a type of REIT that does not list in the stock exchange and shares must be purchased through brokers. Since they are not publicly traded, their shares do not suffer from the volatility that REITs traded on exchanges experience. This essentially means that investing in non-traded REITs is similar to investing directly in real estate since the price of the shares are driven by the net asset value of their portfolio.

However, the reason why these REITs do not experience volatility is because of their lack of liquidity. Investors cannot simply sell their shares the way they could with a public REIT since there is a holding period of eight years or longer. Although some private REITs do allow for early redemption, this may be at a discount, meaning that the investor could lose part of their investment.

Thus, the shares of private REITs tend to hold their value. According to research published in the University of Texas's research publication Texas Enterprise, in 2009 the share value of non-traded REITs declined by only 15% while that of exchange-traded REITs fell by some 67 percent

However, there are a number of drawbacks and risks when investing in non-traded REITs. For instance, they are known for charging high fees due to broker commissions and other upfront fees, which can be as much as 15% of the offering price. The initial distributions may also come from the proceeds of the offering, which includes the principal of the investors, since the REIT may not yet be generating significant income in its early stages.

In addition, many non-traded REITs are structured such that they must either go public at the end of a certain period or must liquidate. If it goes public, the investors' shares are replaced with new ones that may have a lower value than the original. If it liquidates, then the investor may end up with the value of their investment greatly decreased.

Thus, if you are considering investing in non-traded REITs, you should be sure to do your homework by finding out as much as you can about it. You should acquire the REIT's prospectus, which is an offering document in which they provide information such as the offering terms and investing strategy. These are available through your broker or from the EDGAR database of the SEC, which usually identifies them as a 424B3 filing.

REIT ETFs

These investment instruments are alternatives to directly investing in REITs. These exchange-traded funds invest in REITs that are designed to mirror the performance of REIT indexes such as the Dow Jones US REIT Index and the MSCI US REIT Index. Since these ETFs represent a diversified portfolio of REITs of different types of real estate, there is less risk that their profitability will be affected by market shifts.

The largest REIT ETFs include:

- Vanguard Real Estate ETF. This fund tracks the performance of the MSCI US REIT Index and its holdings include some of the largest REITs in the market, such as Crown Castle International, Simon Property Group and American Tower.
- Shwab US REIT ETF. This fund mostly invests in REITs included in the Dow Jones US Select REIT Index, although it may also include others not listed as well.
- iShares US Real Estate ETF. This fund mostly invests in REITs that are included in the Dow Jones US Real Estate Index. Although its holdings emphasize large cap companies, they may also include medium and small cap companies.

In addition, more adventurous investors may consider REIT ETFs that invests in real estate outside of the US. One example is the Vanguard Global ex-US Real Estate ETF, which tracks the performance of the S&P Global ex-US Property Index, including real estate stocks from over 30 countries.

Pros and Cons of Investing in REITs

When you are considering investing in REITs, the main thing to remember is that you are essentially becoming a real estate owner, with the advantages and disadvantages that brings. Here is a quick overview of the pros and cons of buying REIT shares.

Pros

- **REITs are required to distribute the bulk of their earnings as dividends**. This is one of the main reasons that investors are attracted to REITs, particularly those that are looking for an income-generating investment.
- **The REIT is able to avoid being double taxed.** A corporation is taxed on the profits it earns, and when it pays out part of these as dividends, the recipients also have to pay tax on them. But since REITs don't report a profit and distribute the majority of their income, they are not charged corporate income tax. This means that the after-tax dividends you receive on the REITs will be higher compared with those from stocks issued by corporations.
- **REITs are managed by real estate professionals.** This means that the properties will be professionally managed, maximizing the amount of revenue they generate.
- **REITs are easy to liquidate.** Unlike physical real estate, which can be difficult to turn into cash since the process of finding a buyer and completing the paperwork to finalize the sale can take weeks or even months. On the other hand, you can easily dispose of your REIT shares if you should suddenly need cash.
- **Real estate is the underlying asset of the REITs.** Of course, the value of real estate can fluctuate based on market conditions. But in general, the value of real estate, particularly commercial properties, goes up over the long term. This means that your investment will retain its value.
- **REITs make it easy to diversity your portfolio.** If you bought a property, your money would be tied up in it until you could resell it or it started to generate income. On the other hand, by investing in REIT shares, you can own a diversified portfolio of properties that would already start earning you money. In addition, REITs allow your portfolio to be exposed to another asset class apart from the traditional stocks and bonds.

Cons

- **REITs are vulnerable to market downturns.** If there is an economic slowdown, for instance, occupancy rates for retail properties may decline, affecting the income they generate. Thus, the dividends you receive from your shares will also fall
- **The value of the REIT shares themselves may also decline.** This can be due to factors related to the property market, but share prices can also fall as a result of the decline of the overall stock market.
- **REITs are still subject to taxation**. Although the income generated by REITs are exempt from corporate tax, the company still has to pay real estate taxes. When real estate prices rise, this can significantly increase tax expenses and reduce the revenues available for distribution.
- **REIT dividends do not enjoy preferential tax rates.** REIT dividends are taxed as ordinary income rather than as dividends. This means that they will not be taxed the 15% dividend rate, but a much higher one.

- **There is little money available for further investment.** Since the majority of the REITs income is distributed, there is little left over that can be reinvested in the business. This may require the company to borrow money if it wants to purchase additional properties.

Scoring REITs

A. Liquidity

Since REITs are traded on major stock exchanges, they are very easy to liquidate, compared with actually owning physical real estate. As of 2017, there are 222 REITs with total market capitalization of over $1 trillion. Only physical cash at the bank is more liquid than this!

9/10

B. Scalability

REITs are very scalable since you only need to buy more shares if you want to invest more. On the other hand, if you want to buy more real estate, it is a cumbersome process that requires a lot of time, money and potentially more land.

10/10

C. Potential Return on Investment

When it comes to return on investment, REITs on average provide higher returns than rental income from direct real estate investment. According to data from the NAREIT REITwatch, REITs have returned over 12% a year from 1977 to 2010, compared with private real estate funds, which had returns of 6% to 8% over the same period. In addition, from 2012 to 2017, REITs had a 9% average annual return compared with direct real estate investment, which was at an average annualized rate of around or below eight percent.

As far as taxes go, REIT dividends are taxed as ordinary income and the shareholder has to pay at their highest marginal tax rate. Rental income is taxed as personal income, although you can deduct the expenses related to refurbishing it in preparation for being rented out, as well as maintenance costs.

Most importantly, you can **depreciate the cost of your residential property over 27.5 years**. The depreciation deduction is tax-free, meaning that you can subtract this amount from your rental income and only the difference, if any, is taxable.

In addition, when the shareholder shares their REIT holdings, they are taxed based on whether there has been a capital gain or loss. However, if they have held their shares for more than a year, they can be taxed at long-term capital gains rates, which are smaller.

The same reduced tax rates are applied for those who hold their properties for longer than a year. However, if you flip in less than a year, your profits will be considered short-term capital gains and taxed at the regular income tax rate.

However, REITs are vulnerable to interest rate increases, which can cause dividend yields to decrease. This is because, as interest rates rise, all else being equal, the income produced by REITs at the current stock price is worth less, and so prices generally fall in order to increase the yield of those stocks relative to other income producing instruments. Thus, the accepted wisdom is that investors should sell their REITs when the Fed is raising interest rates.

But real estate is also susceptible to market downturns, which can affect their rental income if they cannot find tenants. And there are costs such as property taxes and maintenance costs, which you will have to shoulder whether or not your property is generating income.

Overall, however, you will enjoy a higher rate of return on REITs compared with direct real estate investment.

8/10

D. Passivity

REITs are a great source of passive income compared with being a property owner (which requires you to be more hands on). Your dividends will be sent to your home as soon as they are paid out, usually in the form of a check or a direct deposit to your account. The only thing that is potentially more passive than this is the interest you earn on your money in the bank - this is why REITs received a passivity score of 90% in this book as well as in the book Passive Income Ideas – 50 Ways to Make Money Online Analyzed.

9/10

E. Simplicity

This criterion refers to how easy it is to get started with this investment. All you need to do to invest in REITs is simply to buy shares in the one you've chosen. Most REITs do not require a minimum investment although the broker may require that you buy shares in blocks of 10 or 100. The broker may also require you to maintain a minimum amount in your trading account.

In addition, many REITs also give you the option to automatically reinvest your dividends in additional shares, although you will still have to pay taxes on them. Reinvestment will allow you to compound your returns over time, substantially increasing the value of your investment. In addition, since the value of the REIT shares can also increase over time, they will pay out higher dividends.

The only difficulty with investing in REITs is choosing which ones to invest in. This will require you to have some knowledge of how to analyze them.

7/10

Ten Tips for Successfully Investing in REITs

1. Stick with equity REITs unless you develop a higher tolerance for risk. If you are an ordinary investor who is just looking for high returns, REITs are a good choice particularly if you are willing to hold on to them for the long-term. But unless you are willing to accept a high level of risk, you should not be tempted by the high returns promised by mortgage REITs.

2. Be forward thinking when you are choosing your REITs. Instead of simply considering where the real estate market is now, look at **where it will be in the future**. For instance, ask what the real estate trends will be in the medium-term, and buy REITs that invest in them. What will be the most popular types of real estate?

3. Consider what the economic conditions will be since these can affect the real estate market. To illustrate, in a recession the income from REITs that focus on industrial and office properties may suffer as their tenants go out of business. On the other hand, retail and residential REITs may be more resilient to hard times.

4. Avoid buying into newly established REITs. These REITs have not yet established a track record so there is no reliable way for you to determine how they perform. For instance, you cannot determine how the REIT maintains its payouts over time. You also cannot tell how the REIT manages changes in interest rates.

5. Avoid buying REITs when the prices are on an uptrend. The reason for this is simple: if the REIT suffers from price volatility, the price could go down below the level you bought it at, resulting in a loss. Instead, look for REITs whose prices have hit their floor price and thus, are on an upswing. This advice is applicable not just to REITs but also stocks.

6. Learn to assess the REIT using the income statement. Net income figures can be deceptive since they may include depreciation expenses, which reduce net income. However, property values often appreciate, which makes it inferior for evaluating performance. Instead, look at funds from operations (FFO), where depreciation is excluded. FFO can be found in the footnotes.

7. Hold your REIT shares in your retirement accounts. If you are planning to save for retirement, REITs are a great way to do so. If you have an IRA Roth account, you will pay taxes on the dividends up-front, but enjoy tax-free disbursements when you reach retirement age. In the meantime, the dividends you placed into the account compound on a tax-free basis. You can also enjoy some tax benefits with traditional REITs, since you may be in a lower tax bracket when you retire.

8. Check the REIT's growth potential by looking at its portfolio of holdings. You can usually find this information on their websites. In particular, look at who the REIT's top tenants are and how many properties they are renting, as well as where they are located. Try to avoid REITs whose tenants are too concentrated in one industry and focus on those whose properties are located in areas with flourishing economies. This will **help you predict what the cash flow and stock price of the REIT will be in the future.**

9. Look at the price of the REIT shares relative to its funds from operations (FFO). If the price-to-FFO multiple is too high, it may indicate that the REIT is overvalued, and the price may experience a big drop. You can compute this multiple by dividing the price by the FFO. How high is too high? You can look at the average multiples from the particular sector the REIT is in to see if the multiple is higher or lower.

10. Make sure that you get help from financial professionals. The tax implications of REITs can be very complicated so to make sure that you are able to fully benefit from your investments, you should consult with an accountant. Of course, you should still do your due diligence on the accountant's advice since your tax returns are ultimately your responsibility.

Interesting Fact #2

The famous Las Vegas strip is for the most part not located in the city of Las Vegas. To avoid tax, it's in a city known as "Paradise" – which is completely surrounded by Las Vegas!

Chapter 2

Real Estate Investment Groups

Real estate investment groups (REIG) have become a popular alternative in recent years to real estate investment trusts. Both allow you to enjoy the benefits of investing in real estate without the effort and time required for direct ownership. They also allow you to start investing without requiring you to have a lot of knowledge about real estate.

However, joining a REIG provides you with an opportunity to learn the ins and outs of real estate investing. This knowledge can be valuable to you later on should you decide to buy your own investment properties.

REIGs are associations of investors who pool their money to invest in real estate, buying, and/or developing properties. They then rent these properties out to generate rental income from them. This income is shared among the investors.

These groups usually specialize in a certain property type, such as commercial or residential real estate. They may also focus on finding properties nationally or concentrate on local real estate investments.

REIGs usually hire professionals to manage and maintain the properties as well as to find tenants. Mortgage payments come from rental income. If there are vacancies, the group may put aside a certain portion of their earnings to cover the shortfall.

REIGs are not the same as real estate investment clubs, although some people use the terms interchangeably. A real estate investment club does not invest in properties. It is simply a networking and educational group that allows members to share expertise about real estate investments. They also help each other find investment opportunities.

These groups are formally incorporated as legal entities, with each member listed as a joint owner. When the group makes a purchase, its official name is what is listed on the deed. Although there are no legal minimums or limits on membership, these groups usually only accept a manageable number, which may be around five to ten members.

They are run based on formal operating rules that the members have agreed on. Like any organization, most of them elect members as officers with specific responsibilities in the running of the group. Members will also jointly make investment decisions, voting on which properties to buy or to sell.

Pros and Cons

The main advantage of joining a REIG is that it allows you to invest in properties for a relatively small amount, although your investment will be larger than when you buy into real estate investment trusts. In exchange, however, the potential earnings will be higher.

Another advantage is that, collectively, the group is pooling its investment capital. This gives them the ability to place bids for properties that, as individuals, they may not be able to bid for.

In addition, REIGs also allow certain underrepresented groups to benefit from property investing. For instance, there are women's real estate clubs and clubs that are designed to teach minorities how to invest in real estate and to accumulate assets. This is to empower them to actually get into the market themselves.

Some groups may also provide education for their members by hosting events in which speakers talk about various investment topics. This may be useful to members who want to learn more about the subject and improve their skills. These gatherings are also invaluable for networking purposes as it allows members to meet and interact with other potential investors.

However, members may be asked to pay an entry fee in addition to their initial investment. They may also be asked to pay recurring annual fees. These fees may ultimately affect your net earnings.

In addition, your investment is not liquid. If you suddenly need to get your money back, you cannot just sell your share. You have to follow the guidelines of the organization as to how to liquidate your investment. This might require that another member buy you out. When this happens, you will have effectively withdrawn from the group since you no longer have any investment in it.

The collective way that decisions are made may also pose a problem. The various members may vote on their decisions based on emotional factors, and this could affect the profitability of the group. For instance, one member may convince the others to vote to hold on to a property that is not generating sufficient income, for sentimental reasons.

How to Choose a Group

Before you decide to invest in a REIG, you should be familiar with what your investment goals are. A REIG holds on to property over the long term in order to generate income from it. If you are expecting to see quick returns on your investment, i.e. by flipping the property, you should not invest in this group.

On the other hand, if you are preparing for retirement, then you should definitely consider investing in a group. This investment will provide you with a recurring source of income for when you are no longer earning income from employment.

When you contact the group, ask about their history. Have they been operating for some time, or are they just getting organized?

If they are a new group, ask about the other members. What experience do they have? If they are all new investors, who is guiding the group as to what investments they should make?

If they are an existing group that is looking for new members, ask about their record. How successful have they been with their investments over time? Ask if you can talk with former members about their experiences with the club.

Ask them about their portfolio of properties. They don't have to give you specifics, just what type of properties they generally invest in. Find out how much you can potentially earn by investing in the group and how often the returns are paid out.

Also consider: who are the members? Is the membership focused on a certain demographic, i.e. older adults, or are they open to anybody? How does the composition of the group affect its investment decisions?

Next, look at the costs of membership. How much does it cost to invest in the group? After your initial investment, do you have to make additional investments?

Also ask about the fees the group charges. Are there entry fees? Are there any recurring fees such as service fees? How are they charged? Are they fixed amounts or a percentage of the profits? Can you offset these fees from your earnings or do you have to pay them separately? Or do you have the option to choose?

What are your obligations as a member? Are there certain duties and responsibilities that you have to fulfill as a member of the group? Does the group meet regularly? Do you have to participate when it has to make investment decisions?

Another important consideration is the group's investment goals. Does the group invest in the type of real estate properties that you are interested in? What is their investment strategy? Is it an aggressive or a conservative one?

If the group offers you access to invest in wholesale properties, do they have documentation attesting to the quality of these assets?

What about exiting the group? What if you want to withdraw your investment? How long do you have to maintain your investment before you can exit? Are there fees and penalties for early withdrawal?

Now that you know what to look for, how do you find a group? Before you start, keep in mind that, generally, REIGs are not regulated in the US unless they have more than $25 million in assets. So, you will have to do your homework to avoid signing up with a group that is not reputable.

The best way to find a trustworthy group is to look for a trade association of investment groups. For instance, there is the National Real Estate Investors Association, which includes investors' groups among its membership. The websites of these groups usually allow you to do a search to find a group in your area.

You can also do a Google search for real estate investment groups, but this is more time-consuming. In addition, the results usually also include real estate investment clubs. But if you have the patience and the search engine skills, this can also be effective.

If you are doing your own research, you might want to check out if the group has a listing and ranking at the Better Business Bureau website. For your own security, go with a group that has the highest A+ rating.

If you know any realtors or real estate dealers in your area, you can also ask them to recommend a group. This is the best way, since you can talk to them about your requirements so that they can suggest a group that best meets them.

Forming Your Own Investment Group

If you can't find a real estate investment group in your area that suits your requirements, you might want to consider forming your own group. Of course, this will take a lot of time and effort on your part, but the potential rewards will be substantial.

Unless you already have some prospects in mind, you should start by joining a real estate investment club. This will allow you to network and find potential members of your club. You can also start to learn about how to invest and what properties to invest in.

Joining a club may also provide you with the opportunity to meet with members of existing investment groups so that you can get an idea of how they work. You can also learn from their mistakes so you can avoid them in your own investment activities.

When assessing potential members, some of the considerations to keep in mind include:

- Do you feel comfortable entrusting them with your money?
- Do you feel that they are responsible enough to pay their contributions on time?
- Will they be able to meaningfully contribute to the group?
- Are they decisive enough to 'pull the trigger' when it comes to making investment decisions?

Aside from looking for potential partners, you should think about how your group will be run. For instance, how much will you need as an initial investment so that you can start buying properties? How many members will you accept and how much will you require them to invest?

You should also consider your investment goals. What types of property do you want to invest in? What investment strategy are you going to follow? You should look for members whose investment outlooks reflect yours.

Once you have identified potential members with similar investment goals who are willing to join your club, invite them for an organizational meeting. Discuss with them how the group will be run and will be organized. For instance, what officer positions will the organization have (President, Vice-President, Treasurer, et. al.)?

You should also discuss how much each person will invest, how withdrawals or reductions of investments will be handled and how the group will be dissolved. Can a person make an initial investment and then pay smaller monthly amounts?

You should also decide how and why to accept new members. For instance, if one of the founders withdraws, will you accept a new member or just increase the remaining members' investments? Under what circumstances will you accept new members?

In addition, if you already have an investment property in mind, you can propose it to them. Make sure to provide details such as the cost of the property, how much is the down payment and how big the mortgage will be.

When you have decided on policies regarding how the group will be run, these should be written down. This document will serve as your operating agreement. All members should agree with its provisions and sign the document in order to make it binding.

Having a binding operating agreement means that you have a formal set of rules that dictates how the company will be run. Thus, you can avoid misunderstandings since you already have written specific guidelines for how to deal with particular issues. Keep this in mind when you are drafting the operating agreement.

Here are some of the things that should be covered:

- What is each member's ownership share (in percent)?
- What are the responsibilities of members?
- What are their duties?
- What are their voting rights?
- How will profit and loss be allocated?
- How will meetings be held?
- How will the company be managed?
- What are the provisions if a member wants to sell his share? What if a member wants to buy out another's share? What if a member wants to sell his share to an outsider?
- What happens if a member dies?

Once you have created an operating agreement and an organizational structure, you can start preparing to register your group. Generally, investment groups are organized as general partnerships, under which all partners will equally share the assets and profits of a business as well as its legal and financial liabilities.

For the purposes of investing, it is best that you register your group as a limited liability company or LLC. Under this type of corporate structure, the partners are not personally liable for the company's debts. This means that creditors cannot sue to seize your personal assets so they can be paid back.

Another advantage of the LLC is that you will enjoy taxation benefits. Since the LLC is considered a pass-through entity, it passes on its profits and losses to the members. Each member is then required to report his profits, paying taxes at personal federal tax rates, rather than as corporate tax.

The LLC thus allows you to avoid double taxation on the rental income. In addition, if you were to dispose of the investment property after a year, it would be also be taxed at the lower capital gains rate.

Another benefit of an LLC is that it allows you the freedom to distribute profits, unlike in a corporation where they have to be given out based on the amounts invested. Thus, you can have a partner who does not make a direct financial investment, but who has agreed to handle the running and maintenance of the properties in exchange for a share of the profits.

It should be noted, however, that the LLC does not exist in perpetuity unlike a corporation. If a member dies or goes bankrupt, the LLC has to be dissolved. In this case, the partners will have to create a business continuation agreement, which will transfer the member's interest to another party to ensure that the company can continue.

Although it is possible to file your own LLC documents, you might want to consult with a lawyer or legal service to help you. This way, you are assured that you will not miss anything that could make your LLC registration invalid. There are many low-cost and reputable legal services, such as Nolo, that you can find online.

In addition, you will have to apply for an Employer Identification Number (EIN) with the IRS. The EIN is a unique nine-digit number that also indicates in which state the business is registered. You can apply for one at the IRS website by filling up an application form. You do not have to pay for anything as registration is free.

All businesses need to have an EIN as this allows the IRS to identify them for the purposes of filing business taxes. Financial institutions such as banks and brokerages will also not allow you to open an account if you do not have an EIN.

When you register your LLC, you should include your operating agreement in the registration papers. It is not mandatory in most states, but if you do not file one, it is construed to indicate your agreement to run your group based on your state's default rules. These are very broad since they are not tailored to a particular business and may not be appropriate for your particular requirements.

Another thing you need to do is to open a bank account in the name of the business. You will have to designate people who will have direct access to this account – usually the treasurer or other officer. The company's money will be deposited into this account and disbursed as needed.

One of the keys to the success of the group is keeping accurate records. By doing so, you can account for each members' share of the equity as well as their returns. This will help you avoid misunderstandings that can result in conflict within the group.

You can prepare your records using a Google spreadsheet with the relevant data on it. You can even make it accessible to the other members to ensure the transparency of the group's financial affairs.

If you are inexperienced, you might want to consult with a professional accountant. They will show you how to keep records, what documents you need to keep, and most importantly, how to file your tax returns. The cost of hiring one will be more than offset by the potential penalties from the IRS that you will be able to avoid.

Unless one or more of the members are willing to take on the job of managing and maintaining the property, the group will have to hire somebody to do it. You and the other members will have to decide how much to pay them and how they will be paid. If the property is not yet generating income, you will have to shoulder their salary out-of-pocket. The members may have to make donations until the rental income starts to come in.

Once there are candidates, the members will have to approve them, unless a particular member is designated with the power to hire. Either way, once a particular person or persons are hired, there will have to be a meeting so that the members will be familiar with them.

Scoring REIGs

A. Liquidity

Your investment is not liquid since it is not easy to withdraw it if you suddenly need money. Unlike REITs, you cannot simply sell your share. Depending on the bylaws of the group, you may need to ask another member if they are willing to buy out your share.

2/10

B. Scalability

This depends on the rules of the group. Usually, however, you cannot just increase your investment unless the group decides to buy another property. If you want to increase your investment in real estate, you may have to join another group.

2/10

C. Potential Return On Investment

As with real estate investment trusts, the ROI earned with REIGs comes from both rental income and your share of the proceeds if the property is sold. Thus, the return on investment can vary depending on how much income is generated.

There are other factors that may affect your profitability. For instance, the group may impose other fees and charges, such as your share of management and maintenance costs.

On the other hand, it should be noted that real estate investments are still among the most profitable. Provided that the group chose its investment well, then you should still enjoy a high ROI even after expenses are removed. You will also be able to pay fewer taxes if you organize your group as an LLC.

5/10

D. Passivity

Investing with a real estate investment group is not passive income since it requires some effort. The amount of effort required depends on whether you join a group or form your own. However, it still requires less effort than direct ownership since you can share duties with others. In addition, once the property has started generating income, the effort required to continue earning income will be sharply reduced.

5/10

D. Simplicity

How easy is it to get into investing through a group? Again, it depends. If you are setting up your own group, then it is not simple. But if you are just joining one, it may be as simple as just attending meetings and making your investment.

Be that as it may, you do not need a high level of expertise when you invest with a group. In fact, it is designed for people who are not that knowledgeable about investing, since you will have the benefit of more experienced investors working with you.

5/10

Ten Tips for Successfully Investing in REIGs

1. Make sure that you feel comfortable with the other members of the group. Whether you join a group or form your own, keep in mind that you are ultimately entrusting the success of your investment to other people. So it is very important that you trust them and feel comfortable with them handling your money. This way, you will have peace of mind that your investment is in good hands.

2. Take a long-term viewpoint. As mentioned earlier, REIGs follow a buy-and-hold strategy that involves holding on to the investment property to generate income from it. It may take some time before you start earning the maximum returns from your investment. So you should be patient. Don't expect to start earning a lot from your investment at once.

3. Keep learning. Real estate investment clubs should never be just about making money. They should also provide an opportunity for members to constantly learn new things about investing. If you run the group, make sure that you provide educational opportunities such as inviting speakers and holding workshops. This will help them to make better decisions when you have to vote on your investments and ultimately make them more profitable.

4. Build a network. One of the most important functions of joining a REIG is not just being able to pool your money to invest, but meeting people who can help you. Through the group, you can find a mentor who will help you learn about investing and avoiding common mistakes. You can also build a support group with whom you can brainstorm ideas and talk over your problems.

5. Be disciplined with your commitments to the group. You should not view your participation in the REIG as simply a way to make money. Make sure that you allocate time to meet your duties and responsibilities. Keep in mind that the success of the group would ultimate result in greater profitability of your investment.

6. Periodically assess the strategy of the group. Take time to meet with the other members and discuss investments. Are you maximizing your investment with this property? Should you add another property or sell the one you have? Should you shift (i.e. pivot) to another type of property? Is the management strategy maximizing the returns the group gets from the property? Does the group need to change or adjust its strategy?

7. Work with an accountant. Unfortunately, our tax laws are very complicated and there is a possibility that you may miss something that will result in severe penalties later on. A qualified accountant can help you avoid these pitfalls. And the costs of hiring one will be more than offset by the savings you can enjoy long-term.

8. Make the meetings enjoyable. You should not treat your group meetings as if it was a board meeting of a corporation. Of course, there are serious parts, such as reporting on the state of the investments. At the same

time, you should remember that you are also networking with the other members. Make sure that you provide snacks and refreshments. You can also schedule social activities for the members, such as going golfing.

9. Don't be afraid to leave if you have to. If the group no longer fulfills your investment requirements, you should not hesitate to exit. Of course, this can be difficult, particularly if you have already become fond of the other members. But keep in mind that there are other ways that you can support the group, such as becoming a mentor to new members or by being a regular speaker.

10. Have an exit strategy. There may be times when the group decides that it is better to sell the property to a bigger investor rather that continue to run it. You should already have prepared for this possibility by creating a plan for wrapping up the group. How will you wrap up the group's affairs? How will the proceeds of the sale be divided among the members?

Interesting Fact #3

The primary purpose of a Castle's moat was to prevent attackers from digging tunnels under the walls.

Chapter 3

Real Estate Limited Partnership

Partnership is a form of business entity that exists in numerous industries, not just in real estate. It has two classifications: general and limited. In general partnerships, two or more parties join together and contribute their resources for a venture. These resources include, but are not limited to, skills, labor, money, equipment and land. All the parties involved (known as partners) have their own roles and can exercise control on the various operations of the business.

If they have no written agreement about unequal profit and role distribution, they would share the gains and losses together. Every partner also has the same limitless personal liability for debts and litigations involving the venture.

In contrast, limited partnership, as its name implies, have definite boundaries regarding the contribution of each partner and the distribution of profits and liabilities. In this setup, the one party that does more gets more and has more power compared to the other party. However, the other party can gain from the venture without spending much time and effort. His personal liabilities are limited and risk exposure is low as well.

Each partner in general partnership should be knowledgeable in operating a business. On the other hand, limited partnership doesn't require everyone to be familiar with the nature of the business. This makes real estate limited partnership (RELP) an ideal investment choice for anyone who wants to invest in the real estate industry despite not having sufficient knowledge or training on property development and management.

Overview of Business Model

Limited partnership is more common in the real estate industry than in any other industry. It's mainly because property development and management require significant amount of capital investments. Other businesses can be financed through loans because they have securities to offer. The real estate can be used as securities for loans, but doing so usually complicates property management. The interests can eat up the potential profits as well.

RELP is similar with REIT and REIG in the sense that it raises capital by getting investors. Unlike the two, however, limited partnership is less complex. It may also be restricted to a small group. One family or group of friends can even pool their money, select a property manager, and set up a RELP.

In RELP, there are at least two parties involved. They're classified as either general or limited partner. Real estate developers and property managers are the ones who serve as general partners. Limited partners, on the other hand, could be any person or business.

The General Partner

Purchasing raw land, developing properties, converting lands, financing real estate deals and selling developed lands are among the functions of real estate developers. They usually start with planning what kind of property to develop; it could be a condominium building, an apartment complex, a planned community or a shopping center. If the developer gets capital investments from limited partners, the properties they tend to develop are those that can be sold.

Before making proposals to would-be limited partners, developers scour the state or country for raw or developed lands where they can turn their plans into reality. Upon making a shortlist, they make an offer to buy the lands from the respective owners. The sale rarely happens overnight. It may take numerous negotiations which involve adjusting the proposed amount and adding offers such as relocation.

If the negotiations fail, the developers go for the other options in their shortlists. They'll keep going until a landowner accepts the offer. Prior the transfer of ownership, the developers get capital investments from limited partners and use a portion of that to pay the landowners.

Once all the paperwork regarding the ownership is done, the developers will then start the construction in a raw land. If the land they bought has an existing building, they will begin with demolition. Before the construction gets completed, the developers will market them to potential buyers. The sale of properties determines the amount that each limited partner will get as ROI.

Before the sale of developed properties, the developers hold ownership over them. This is their main difference with property managers. Developers may or may not manage the properties they own. Conversely, property managers may not own the properties they're supposed to rent out or sell.

Independent property managers don't have to buy and develop properties, but they may do some renovation. They're hired by developers, building-owners and homeowners to oversee the sale or lease of properties. Property managers are in charge of dealing with the buyers and tenants directly. They're expected to be familiar with the properties and the surrounding environment because they have to answer queries from prospects. If the buyers and tenants have issues, property managers are also tasked to resolve them.

In RELP, property managers can also get financial investments from limited partners and use such to purchase properties. The limited partners could be deemed as the collective owners of the properties before they get sold. However, they can't live on the said properties or use them in any other way because there's no definite distribution of the properties beforehand.

Between developers and property managers, the former deals with greater risk. Property development involves several steps that take years to be completed. The negotiations alone can take months. Disputes with the owners of neighboring properties may also arise, which will further cause delays and losses. The construction, along with the demolition of existing structure, may be finished within a year provided that the developer has sufficient capital investments.

As a general partner, however, developers are better in offering higher ROIs especially if they handle every aspect of property development (like construction, property management and marketing) instead of outsourcing the services of other companies.

In contrast, independent property managers may only take months to renovate, market and sell properties. But because they didn't have much control over the construction of the property, they have to settle with the existing design. This limits the potential worth of the property.

The Limited Partner

As for the role of a limited partner, it's basically providing capital investments to finance the purchase, development and marketing of properties. In the process, as a limited partner, you're also indirectly paying management fees to the general partner.

Depending on the size of the real estate, there could be one or more limited partners. For limited partners, the number of limited partners shouldn't affect their ROIs. It's the amount of their capital investments that matter. The number of limited partners affects the general partner in different ways, though. If there's only one limited partner, the amount of capital investment may not be that sufficient for the real estate deals.

On the other hand, having more limited partners mean more financial help for the general partner. But this also means that the general partner is financially and legally accountable to more people in case there are violations in the written agreement regarding the RELP.

Limited partners and stockholders are both regarded as investors, but unlike the latter, limited partners have no direct control on the selection, conversion, marketing and other management aspects of the real estate. Stockholders may not have control as well, but because their investments can be liquidated easily, they can influence the management to bend down and heed their demands. Limited partners, on the other hand, don't have such influence.

There are two ways to become a limited partner: the first one is buying limited partnership (LP) units and the other is dealing with a general partner directly. Buying LP units is a lot like buying stocks. You can do it online with the help of brokerage firm or through the stock exchange itself. It's less time-consuming and less risky than setting up a RELP with a general partner. If you choose to buy LP units, you can also benefit from property management involving real estate in different states or even in another country.

Brokerage firms can be strict, though, when it comes to accepting limited partners. They usually set a minimum amount of capital investment. Additionally, you might be required to undergo some training.

If you intend to get LP units from the stock exchange, make sure you are buying the right securities. Otherwise, you won't be able to enjoy the tax benefits for limited partners.

Forming a RELP along with a general partner offers you a chance to suggest properties to manage especially if real estate opportunities abound in your district. A general partner could be any individual, but as much as possible, you should choose someone who has experience in property management. If you opt for this instead of buying LP units, you're not just investing money; you're also investing trust in the general partner. If a problem arises, both your investment and relationship could be affected.

For managing family estates, the members of the family can form a RELP as well. Once the family estate is rented out or sold, the gift and excess taxes that the limited partnership has to pay are lesser compared to the taxes when managing the estate as individuals. Moreover, a RELP offers transparency and helps reduce the possibility of conflicts between family members regarding the distribution of profits. To further ensure fairness, the family can hire a third-party as property manager.

Formation of a RELP

To form a RELP from scratch, you and your would-be general partner should discuss the properties that the latter will manage. You may or may not partake in the researching and planning stages. However, you have the chance to participate in discussing the goals of the limited partnership so you should make the most out of it.

When the business goals and plans are determined, you and your general partner can then decide the name and logo of your RELP. The next step is to set up an office for your general partner. As the registered agent of your venture, an office address is necessary partly because this is where the authorities can send summons to and where prospective buyers can visit.

In most US states, another requirement for registering a RELP is a written agreement between the partners. The written agreement should detail the rights and responsibilities of each party. There should also be information regarding legal and financial sanctions in case one party fails to do his task.

These sanctions should protect the general partner if you, as the limited partner, don't give the amount required for capital investments. Such sanctions should also provide protection for you in case your general partner doesn't give your supposed dividends or allow you to review the venture's accounting records.

The distribution of profits and liabilities should be included in the agreement as well. There should be a target date indicated in the written agreement about the start of putting the properties on sale. This will give you an idea on how long you have to wait before you can get your investment back and earn profits.

To protect himself from unlimited personal liability, the general partner can apply for a limited liability partnership. If the general partner does all the work while you're the only one financing, you may opt for an equal distribution of profits. However, the general partner has the upper hand in altering the distribution after a certain period of time.

Another important component of the written agreement is the clause regarding the process of dissolving the RELP. This one will be useful in mitigating losses in case the property management doesn't work out the way the general partner has planned. The written agreement should be reviewed by a certified public accountant and notarized by a lawyer to prevent loopholes and to make sure it's legally binding.

This may not be necessary but it helps if you include information regarding a possible change in ownership structure. This will become useful when you're not satisfied with your general partner's management style. You may choose to take over some of his roles and rights as general partner based on the clause on changing ownership structure. Doing so, however, entails that you're no longer a limited partner so you'll be no longer eligible for the tax benefits, lower risk exposure and limited personal liability.

Aside from the written agreement, the general partner has to secure the necessary permits, licenses and certifications required in the state where the office is located. Once settled, the general partner can then file for a certificate of limited partnership in the office of the local secretary of the state. This involves paying for filing fees. Registering for business tax is the next step.

Some RELPs opted to register in another state instead of where their office is. This is a strategy to avoid costly filing fees especially in states where there's a real estate boom. Tax incentives are also better in some states which serve as their way of attracting investors. To apply your RELP in another state, though, you and your general partner need to comply with the foreign qualifications set by the state.

Before you get the certificate of limited partnership, you can still make suggestions to your general partner. However, once there's a certificate, you shouldn't meddle with the tasks of the general partner in one way or another. Doing so can serve as violation of your written agreement.

Depending on your agreement, the general partner should provide weekly, monthly and yearly updates regarding the gains and losses of your venture. Other than the gains and losses, he has the option not to divulge information about the daily operations of your partnership.

Being the sole limited partner means you'll shoulder the majority—if not all—of the capital investments needed to be raised for your venture. This is a great risk on your part. To minimize such risk, one option is to look for additional limited partners. You can let your general partner do this on your behalf. But if you do so, you shouldn't stop your general partner from accepting or rejecting certain people or business entities.

Ideally, all limited partners will get the same percentage of dividends. However, when a general partner talks to another limited partner, he may offer a deal that's better than the one he has with you.

After a certain period of time, you may re-negotiate with your general partner. He might make additional proposals to entice you to re-invest your dividends to the partnership. It may also be his way of encouraging you to increase your capital investments. If you no longer want to take part in the partnership, you can get out and take your investment elsewhere.

During negotiations, the general partner usually presents projected values of the properties. Instead of focusing on the projections, you should ask about the bases for such. Political and economic crisis in the local communities can affect the real estate market.

If the general partner can't justify that the local political and economic scene will maintain its status quo or improve in the future, it might not be better to invest in the said properties. But if the status quo could be maintained or if the prospects are good, the property development and management are ideal investment options.

Pros and Cons

One pro of being a limited partner is that it doesn't require your active involvement in managing the properties. On the other hand, general partners handle many things. It's not surprising that not a lot of people would like to be such. The same goes with being a stockholder in a real estate company or being an owner of a rental property. Thankfully, being a limited partner enables you to earn passively from real estate.

It's also a pro that you don't have to find and convince buyers when you are in a RELP. Not everyone is cut out to be a property manager because such job requires people skills. If you're not too keen on dealing with investors, contractors, landowners, buyers, tenants, and maintenance technicians, being a property manager may not be for you. Nevertheless, you can still gain from RELP thanks to a skilled property manager.

Your personal liability in a RELP is limited. As a limited partner, you still have personal liability over the venture's debts. This means that the authorities and creditors can go after your personal assets. **However, your personal**

liability won't go beyond the amount of your capital investment. Plus, the authorities and creditors usually go after the general partner's assets first. You might still have a bit more time to prepare if they start seizing.

Another good thing about RELP is that the limited partner doesn't have to deal with litigation. Only the general partner has personal liability in case the company gets sued.

You're also not in charge of paying business taxes. The general partner will be the one paying business taxes. The payment may come from your capital investments but at least you won't have to deal with tax preparation and filing.

RELP is less risky compared to other real estate investment options. In RELP, there's always a property to be sold which means that there's a greater chance that you'll be able to get your investment back. After the sale, you can invest elsewhere or re-invest in your partnership which will cover new properties.

It's easier to track your profits and expenses as a limited partner.

A general partner can enjoy management fees and shared profits from the sale of the real estate. However, such advantages come with the complexity of tracking personal gains and losses. As a limited partner, you'll find it easier to identify and compute your profits, making your tax preparation less stressful as well.

You can learn from your general partner. Even if you aren't directly involved in the way the property or your capital investments are managed, you can still observe and learn from your general partner's marketing strategies. You might be able to score some connections for your next investments as well. Being a limited partner can also serve as your training ground in becoming a general partner.

On the downside, you have little to no control on various aspects of the business in a RELP. In a general partnership, the parties involved can make compromises whenever they have disagreements. That can't be said about limited partnership. Limited partners are also referred as silent partners because they don't have a say on how the property is managed. Nevertheless, you won't feel the need to control the business operations if you have a dependable property manager.

As a limited partner, you can't force your general partner to buy a property you like or market it in a certain way. You can't stop him from buying certain properties either. If you're quite close to your general partner, you might be able to recommend properties and marketing strategies. However, the other party still reserves the right to accept or reject your suggestions. In case you just have LP units, your ability to make suggestions is further restricted.

It will take years before you can make some profits. Unless your general partner has plenty of connections to close sales and unless the properties are already developed, you shouldn't expect to gain significant ROIs right away. You're lucky if you get your investment back and earn 15% ROIs after five years.

If the real estate gets sold at a much lower price, you might not be able to recoup your initial investment. Most of the time, the properties involved in RELPs are sold in one way or another. However, the expected value of the property doesn't always turn out to be true.

If this happens, you won't be able to get your investment back. Worse, you might even have to pay for debts in case the sale didn't generate enough money to pay back the venture's debts. The general partner may get debts in case the real estate deals require re-financing. As a limited partner, you can't advise him to avoid such.

The general partner can re-schedule the distribution of dividends. As if the years of waiting aren't enough, the general partner can postpone the distribution of dividends. This won't be much of a disadvantage if the general partner makes a counter-offer such as bigger percentage in the succeeding sales. But if you badly needed that ROI, this will become a major disappointment.

In case the property is sold at a much higher price than the projected one, the general partner may keep the excess for himself. It's a good thing if your general partner is able to meet the expected sale of the property. This means that you'll get your expected ROIs as well.

As for the excess, the general partner can opt not to share it with you. But instead of considering this as a disadvantage on your part, you should think of it as an incentive for the general partner for doing a great job.

There's a risk that your general partner will abandon your venture. Trust is an important element in RELP. Even if your general partner is someone you know personally, there's still the possibility that he will spend all your capital investment and run away without giving your money back. The risk is greater if you're dealing with a general partner you just met for the sake of the venture.

The best way to reduce this risk is get to know your general partner well. Even if you're buying LP units from a brokerage firm, you should still research about the developer or property manager that will use up your capital investments.

If you have doubts about the integrity and/or competency of a potential general partner, it will be much better for you to avoid partnering up with him. Making a deal with them, despite having trust issues, will only result to stress in the long run, whether your doubts are proven right or wrong. If your doubts are proven to be true, your capital investment is also at risk.

Scoring RELPs

A. Liquidity

One of the criticisms with RELPs is that it takes time for every partner to get their investment back. For limited partners, their investments are practically illiquid. It's possible for them to opt out, but getting the exact capital investment right away is another story.

3/10

B. Scalability

Property developments may need re-financing at one point. This will be a good chance for limited partners to increase their investments. However, scaling may not be that easy if there's a certain period of time stated in the written agreement before re-financing and re-negotiations will be entertained.

C. Potential Return On Investment

The earnings of limited partners in RELPs can be substantial and they are considered as securities. Thus, if you're a limited partner, you have to pay for the appropriate taxes for such earnings. Nevertheless, the tax isn't as burdensome as business and estate tax.

8/10

D. Passivity

Of all real estate investment options, nothing can beat RELP in terms of earning passively. Your only task is to buy LP units or provide cold cash. Once you're done with this, you can leave everything to the general partner. You can simply look or ask for updates every once in a while.

9/10

E. Simplicity

Whether you buy LP units or form a RELP with someone else, being a limited partner is simpler than being a property manager, stockholder or landlord. The major challenges with this investment option are to find a reliable RELP and be accepted as a limited partner.

8/10

Tips for Successfully Investing in RELPs

1. Choose a general partner who has a proven track record of selecting and managing properties that offer high ROIs.

2. Start investing in a RELP that focuses more on developing residential properties.

3. If you want quicker returns, invest in properties that are already constructed. If you want higher returns, look for properties that are still in the process of getting completed.

4. Diversify your RELP investments. Make sure there are short-term and long-term RELPs.

5. Avoid "handshake" agreements even if the general partner is a family, friend or colleague. Always have a written partnership agreement that's properly accounted and notarized.

6. Prioritize buying LP units from a reliable brokerage firm instead of giving cold cash and setting up a RELP from scratch.

7. Never step out of your boundaries as a limited partner. If you try to get involved in any of the daily operations of your partnership, you might lose your status as limited partner and incur additional liabilities in the process.

8. Partner up with one general partner and several limited partners for one venture.

9. Never invest more than what you can afford to lose.

10. If RELP is just a single investment opportunity for you, you can do it with a small group like your family or friends. If you intend to make it as a recurring investment, go for an established firm.

Interesting Fact #4

In Japan, most houses *depreciate in value*. Half of all houses are demolished within 38 years and there is virtually no market for pre-owned homes. Per capita, there are nearly four times as many architects and more than twice as many construction workers in Japan as the U.S.

Chapter 4

Tax Lien Certificates

Many real estate investors allocate a portion of their investment portfolio to tax lien certificates. They find it wise to invest in these instruments owing to the relatively low entry point and safety.

Tax lien certificates are issued on properties with unpaid property taxes. They can be acquired through auctions. Depending on the rules, a bidder wins by offering either the lowest interest rate or the highest premium over the amount of the lien.

The winning bidder pays the government in cash for the amount of tax liability on the property. He receives his tax lien certificate and can expect to be paid by the property owner an amount equivalent to the lien plus the interest before a specified expiration date.

This investment instrument is favorable to the government and to the investor. The government is able to effectively collect on property taxes by offering lien certificates to willing investors. For investors, on the other hand, these are simple and safe instruments that can give them modest returns over a term of 3-5 years.

How Tax Liens Work

Property taxes are used to fund the salaries of school teachers, policemen, firemen, and other public officials and employees in many counties and territories. Tax revenues are also used to build infrastructure.

When property owners do not pay their taxes, it follows that the government will not have a source of funds for all its essential expenses. This is why the government needs to issue tax liens on properties whose owners go delinquent on their tax obligations.

Liens are issued by the government and tax lien auctions are held periodically. There are on-location auctions and online auctions. Investors bid on these liens either in terms of interest rate or of premium top up. The government issues tax lien certificates that indicate the amount of tax to be settled, the interest due, and the expiration date.

It is important to note that not all states offer tax liens. There are some states that sell the property straight out. In states that do issue tax liens, the government offers investors a chance to earn when the taxes are paid by the property owner or future buyer on or before a specified date.

The property owner is obligated to pay the tax lien within the stipulated period. Otherwise, the property may be foreclosed. Either way, the tax lien certificate investor does not have to worry about as he is assured of payment.

The security of a tax lien certificate comes from it being higher in priority ranking in terms of payments. Even in a mortgage foreclosure, the holder of the tax lien certificate is paid first before payments are applied to other financial obligations and expense lines.

Investing in Tax Lien Certificates

One of the factors that make tax lien certificates appealing to investors is their affordability. The purchase amount can be as low as a few hundred dollars for small properties to thousands of dollars for bigger and more attractive properties. Investors buy tax lien certificates from auctions by placing bids on:

- ❖ **Interest** – the maximum interest rate is set by each county. They can be as low as 12% to as high as 50%. The interest rates are printed on the tax lien certificates and are considered to be binding.
- ❖ **Premium**– the bidders may ask to pay a specified amount of premium on top of the tax lien. This may or may not earn interest to be paid back to the investor within the redemption period.

The certificate also indicates the redemption period within which the property owner should settle the full amount of his financial obligation. This is usually about 2 to 5 years.

The Auction Process

The tax lien auction is a fairly simple process, but you have to be prepared for it. You need to understand what you are getting into as well as the various factors that affect the market. As yields on tax liens certificates are pretty much set in auctions, you do not have to worry about market fluctuations and valuations.

You need to do due diligence to make sure that the tax lien certificates that you are considering are worth investing in. It's not always about buying the property with the lowest liens. While future property values do not directly affect how much your tax lien certificates are worth, they do affect your chances of being paid back.

Find out what you need to do so you can evaluate your potential yield versus your risks accordingly. Also, be ready with a fall-back position in case things do not go your way during the auction.

Check the auction details in advance to know what is required of you on the day itself. This will also allow you to make quick decisions on properties that you are particularly interested in. For instance, you might have to be prepared to pay up right there and then when you win a bid. Some auctions require full payment within 24 hours while some require upfront payment.

Don't be worried about walking away empty handed. That's alright. Learn from every experience and take each auction as an opportunity to network with other investors. Perhaps these could lead to mutually beneficial partnerships in the future.

Earning From Tax Lien Certificates

There are two possible ways for you to get a return on your investment in tax lien certificates. The first one is, of course, through interest payments. If all works out well and the property owner is able to pay off the lien, you get your money back plus interest.

If, on the other hand, the property owner is not able to make his payments, you can gain from your investment through potential property ownership. However, there are risks and unexpected expenses that could arise out of this scenario. In this case, your gain would depend on how well prepared you are for the risks.

- **When the property owner pays** – you will receive a check within 5 to 10 business days for your investment plus the interest rate. The lien is erased, the property remains with its owner, and you collect on your investment and earnings.

- **When the property owner does not pay** – you may have the property foreclosed and take the amount representing the lien and the interest. Or, you can also take ownership of the house. Your lawyer and the assigned county officials can assist you throughout this process.

Pros and Cons of Tax Lien Certificates

Tax lien certificates are profitable investments. Tax revenue authorities give taxpayers a specific time period within which to settle their obligations on the tax lien certificate. If the taxpayers end up not paying off the debt, then the investor will receive the property deed.

If the owner redeems the property by settling the unpaid balance during the set redemption period, then the investor will receive a profit. You'll get whatever you invested plus the interest earnings. At the very least, you gain a modest amount in interest earnings. At best, you get to own property without paying for its actual market value.

You don't need a huge capital to begin investing in tax lien certificates. Compared to other investment methods, investing in these certificates do not require a huge amount of capital for buying in.

You do not have to fork out thousands of dollars to invest in these certificates as you would for mutual funds and other investment instruments. For just a few hundred dollars, you can already purchase tax lien certificates and look forward to more substantial potential yield.

You can diversify your investments. Because your initial capital is smaller compared to other kinds of investments, you can easily diversify and spread your capital across various multiple tax lien certificates.

Diversification can be done by buying certificates found in various housing markets. Do not limit yourself to just one county. There are various auctions held all across the country. It would be good to do some research on the most profitable areas for investing in tax lien certificates.

It could serve as a source of passive income. While you would have to do some ground work before you invest in this instrument, you can just leave it to earn for you once you've finished setting it up.

There are no market values for you to watch or bids and trades to place to profit from your investment. If you are investing in several certificates, you simply need to get organized and track the redemption periods and expiration dates.

You'll be able to familiarize yourself with the real estate market and take advantage of other investment opportunities it offers. Going to auctions and investing in these certificates is a good way to get your feet wet in the real estate market. There are many other real estate investment instruments for you to put your money in and earn from.

The real estate market is a lucrative market. Aside from tax lien certificates, you can learn all about buying and selling properties, renting out residential and commercial spaces, providing accommodations to transients and long-term tenants, flipping houses, and other similar income-generating activities. Eventually, you can move to other kinds of real estate investments and grow your income earning potential.

Beginner investors should be cautious about plunging into this kind of investment. Although it is relatively safe, it is easy for those who are just starting out to make bad decisions when it comes to which properties to invest in.

Do your homework and learn as much as you can about this instrument. The prep work and the decision-making required for this investment requires deeper understanding of the market and the possible outcomes of investing in tax lien certificates.

For instance, you have to be aware of the risks that you may face if the owner doesn't pay for the taxes and fails to redeem the property. You can end up paying for expensive court costs just to obtain the tax deed and you won't even get profits from your original investment.

Also, if the property owner ends up filing for bankruptcy, you might not be able to push for the foreclosure of the property while the decision on the bankruptcy case is still pending.

Tax liens aren't everlasting instruments. You cannot buy a tax lien certificate and hold on to it for a long time. You cannot expect it to appreciate in value over the long term. It has an expiration date. After this date, any unclaimed and unpaid balances cannot be collected by the investor anymore.

It is also possible for the property to go into foreclosure and the investor could find out that there are other liens issued on it. This means that there are others who can lay claim on the property and it would be difficult to get the property deed or title.

To put it bluntly, you might not get anything from your investment when this happens. Your certificate will not be worth more than the paper it's printed on after its expiration date.

The amount of capital can vary. You need to have cash on-hand to invest in this instrument. Those who are short of cash might not be able to take advantage of this investment instrument even if it only requires a small amount of money to get into.

Be careful not to put in all your cash into this investment. These are not liquid assets that you can convert to cash when you need it. Follow the basic rule that you are not supposed to invest money that you are not prepared to lose.

You could end up spending more on repairs and other related expenses. If you buy a tax lien certificate on a property without checking it out first, you could end up with a property that requires considerable repairs. With such a property, the owner would probably not have any interest in making any more payments at all and could easily 'abandon' it.

This could leave you with a piece of property that's worth less than what you expected. You might have to spend more for the repairs just to get the property marketable again. Even worse is when the property turns out to have been permanently damaged by some natural catastrophe or environmental conditions.

You can prevent this from happening to you by doing your research and due diligence. The extra time and effort you spend check out the properties will be an advantage for you.

The competition can get fierce. You'd find other investors and money managers looking at the best tax liens to purchase. These seasoned market players already know the market well and have a keen eye on which properties to target.

It could be intimidating when you are faced with competitors with more experience and resources. Don't get fazed. You just have to make sure that you exert more effort in learning the ropes. There are actually experts who can guide you in preparing for the auction and planning your investment strategy.

Scoring Tax Lien Certificates

A. Liquidity

A tax lien certificate is not a liquid investment unlike other financial instruments such as stocks, bonds, and bank deposits that can easily be withdrawn, redeemed, or sold.

Once you've bought a tax lien, you've said goodbye to your money. You can't really demand to get your cash back. You can only wait for the property owner to pay the tax lien off, and sometimes it can take a long time for them to settle the amount.

The tax lien will stay in your portfolio until the owner redeems the property or if you foreclose it. Sure, you can sell your tax lien certificate or assign the rights to another party, but it would also take time before you can find a buyer for it. You may even have to sacrifice the interest you've earned if you want to get your principal back.

1/10

B. Scalability

Tax lien certificate investments are quite scalable, as you can just stock up on these certificates, provided you have the funds to buy more of them. It's not impossible to have multiple certificates, especially if you're closely watching the calendar for auctions in the areas you are interested in. You can build your portfolio if you regularly go to these auctions and buy more certificates.

7/10

C. Potential Return On Investment

Investing in tax lien certificates can be financially rewarding, especially if you came in prepared with enough capital to spend on investments. If you perform the necessary research, then you have bigger chances of bringing home profits.

This kind of investment involves taxes, simply because it all starts with the property owner not paying for the right amount of taxes to the government. When you buy the tax lien certificate, you pay the office the necessary amount of taxes owed by the property owner. In this manner, you're paying taxes owed by somebody else.

6/10

D. Passivity

Investing in tax lien certificates take some amount of work especially if you plan to add new ones to your portfolio periodically. This mean always being on the lookout for properties with tax liens that are going to be auctioned soon, going around to 'investigate' the properties that you are interested in, and preparing bids.

You also have to keep track of redemption periods and expiration dates to ensure that you will get your money back. You can choose to partner with someone else to co-manage your tax lien certificates especially if you are new to investing in real estate.

If you are only interested in investing in a few certificates, you can just sit back and see what happens to your investment after you have done your prep work and have set up this portion of your portfolio, you can pretty much just sit back and wait for the property owners to make their payments.

5/10

E. Simplicity

Investing in tax lien certificates is simple enough for those who already have experience in the real estate market. The process is fairly straightforward, but some groundwork needs to be done before the auction date. Novice investors can learn about this investment instrument, but would benefit from advice and guidance from more experienced investors.

It also does not take a lot of cash to invest in tax lien certificates. You can choose to put your money in only a handful of properties that fit your criteria. Even receiving the payout on the certificate is simple as the investor just has to wait for the check in the mail within a few days from the owner's settlement of his obligations.

5/10

Ten Tips for Successfully Investing in Tax Lien Certificates

As you've realized, like any other investment, there are risks that come with tax lien certificates. You may have been promised a good deal of returns, but you still have to be careful in investing on these. To increase your chances of gaining from your investment in tax lien certificates, here are 10 tips to keep in mind:

1. Be aware of the laws of the area you will be operating in. Laws involving real estate vary across jurisdictions, so you cannot assume that what works when investing in tax lien certificates in one location will be the same in another. Check local laws on liens and real estate investing.

Laws can be very specific to each state and even counties can have their own specified rules as well. You don't have to look far, as most laws are found on the county's official website. If you need qualifications, then you can reach out to the county executive office and they'll assist you further.

2. Have the necessary knowledge and connections. If you're going to invest in tax lien certificates, or in any other real estate investment for that matter, you need to study the market and the competition. You can do this on your own by doing research and taking classes or short courses. You can also find an expert to guide you as you 'learn by doing.'

Establishing connections with those who are already in the industry is a good way to familiarize yourself with the real estate market. If there are local trade groups in your area, it would be good to join them and actively participate in their activities. In the process, you pick up tips and benefit from the sharing of experiences and practices among the members of the group.

3. Understand the auction process. If you could, prior to your first bid, you should attend first an auction just to have a feel of the atmosphere. You may have seen one on TV, but the real process can be scary especially to those who are just starting out. It'll be good to see how it looks like before you get into the real action just yet.

All bids are binding, so don't even attempt to go for one just for experience. Some auctions are held at the property itself, while some are held at a courthouse or even at a specific disclosed location. If you know of a foreclosure lawyer, you may consult with him about the auction process.

4. Be familiar with the property you're going to buy. You don't just buy tax lien certificates without knowing the property associated with it. This is to ensure that you're going to collect the money from the property owner.

What if you're going to be sold a dilapidated property in the slums? That's probably not a good idea regardless of the offered interest rate – the property owner probably wouldn't be able, or even be unwilling, to settle the tax owed.

Stay away from properties that have been hit with environmental damage (e.g., hazardous materials, chemical deposits, storm and flooding, etc.). These properties are generally undesirable.

The more you know about the property, area, and condition, the more confident you will be in placing your bids. It would be a gamble to bid on a property that you are not familiar with or that you have not checked out. When you place your bids, remember that you are not there to win your bids at all cost. You want to go for good deals.

5. Understand that you won't always end up owning the property on which the tax lien certificate that you bought was issued. You shouldn't be investing in tax liens if your intention is to own the properties after the redemption period.

The homeowners still have a chance to retain ownership of their property if they pay their financial obligations before the end of the redemption period. In this case, your gain will only be in the form of interest earnings as dictated by your winning bid.

6. Research, research, research. The fact that you have to research can't be emphasized enough. You should do your due diligence and perform research to succeed. Not doing so could cost you a fortune, so you have to be careful. You wouldn't want to purchase a property just to realize that what you've bought is pretty useless and worthless.

You should also study the market you're interested in so that you'll be aware of the price range at which tax lien certificates in this area are usually sold. It will also give you an idea of the competition among other investors.

7. Work with a professional. Investing in tax lien certificates is not recommended for novice investors, but that doesn't mean newcomers can't entirely invest in them. If you're new but you still want to invest in this real estate instrument, ask for the help of a professional. This way, you'll have someone to guide you through the process and to advice you on the best investment moves.

8. Some people consider tax lien certificates as unacceptable, so you have to be prepared to deal with them. As investing in these certificates is a personal decision, it should not matter what others think. While other people might view the act of taking over someone else's debt as immoral, the other perspective presents it as beneficial to both the homeowner and the investor.

You have to be prepared to be the bad guy in case the homeowner cannot pay his obligations and you are forced to file for foreclosure. If you do not have the heart to do this, perhaps you should look at another real estate investment instrument.

9. Understand the responsibilities that come with your investment. Upon receiving the certificates, the property owner should be informed, in writing, of the purchase within a specific amount of time. Another letter of notification should be sent to the property owner once the redemption period is almost over. You should also be aware of the foreclosure laws. Pay attention to provisions that govern the handling of the property when the owner fails to pay his debt.

10. There are risks associated with this kind of investment. There will always be risks associated with investments, and this isn't an exception. Tax lien certificates may not be related to the markets, making them a somehow predictable and stable investment, but there still are factors to consider especially in this field where interest rates are rising. You'd also have to face tough competition, especially when it comes to auctions.

The risks often come with the properties being bought. Again, choosing unwanted properties, or those with little value, can leave you with a land that you'll find hard to make money from. You wouldn't want to lose your principal and not receive interest just because nobody wishes to redeem the property you bought.

Interesting Fact #5

The Buji Khalifa (in Dubai) is so tall that you can watch the sunset from the base of the building, take an elevator to the top, and *watch the sunset all over again*!

Congratulations!

The fourth character of the password required to unlock the *Real Estate Business Scorecard* is letter s.

Chapter 5

Land

Investing in a vacant land is often the most misunderstood and overlooked real estate business model. Many real estate investors would tell you that this is a high-risk real estate investment strategy, and they have some valid arguments.

Basically, a vacant land will not provide you an outright regular income, and you can't just sell it overnight. Buying a vacant land is also not as sexy as buying REITs or investing in REIGs. But once you drill down the intricacies of this business model, you can transform a boring piece of land into an asset that will become a source of your regular cash flow.

For some investors, investing in a vacant land is boring, but for those who know the business, they love the fact that the land is just sitting there. The stability and simplicity of owning the land purchased at the right price could really override the multitude of problems that you have to face with other forms of real estate investments.

It is best first to understand the business model of vacant land investment including its pros and cons so you are equipped with the right knowledge once you encounter this viable real estate opportunity.

Land Investment Business Model

Purchasing a vacant land is just one of the many ways to make money in property investment. However, this form of investment does not actually involve any property at all because you are purchasing only the land. In this form of real estate investment, you are buying a land and holding it for a while in the hope that its value will increase in the future.

Why Does Land Value Increase Over Time?

There are several factors behind the growth of land's market value, which is also known as capital value appreciation. These factors include supply and demand, fiscal inflation, bank interest rates, area development, and population growth.

Supply and Demand

If a demand is increasing for certain types of land in an area, such as residential, agricultural, or industrial, the prices will go up when the volume of real estate projects being developed to sustain the demand doesn't catch up. For example, companies purchasing vacant lots in an area deemed ideal for factories are willing to pay more for lands because establishing factories in the area is great for business.

When it comes to residential areas, the demand from end-users can also attract the attention of investors who are buying residential properties with the perspective of placing them in the market again once the supply in the area decreases and the prices increase.

Fiscal Inflation

Inflation happens when there is a high volume of money in circulation, which causes the value of money to decrease. In this case, the prices of commodities increase including construction materials and the cost of acquiring land. Certainly, fiscal inflation will not lead to increased property prices in an area if the location itself is not sufficient, which means it has poor accessibility, civic and social infrastructure, or there is an oversupply of real estate projects already.

Bank Interest Rates

The variable movement of bank rates has a direct effect on the value of land. If the cost of borrowing increases, the demand for properties slows down because few buyers are willing to purchase lands through bank financing. Similarly, if bank interest rates decrease, more investors are willing to buy properties and so the market sentiment also appreciates. These factors result in a higher demand for land purchase.

Area Development

Especially for residential areas, the value of land could significantly increase if there are current developments in an area such as shopping malls, schools, public transport facilities, government offices, commercial buildings, and more. You should also check the zoning regulations in the area to see if there are limits on excessive development.

Population Growth

Obviously, the more people who are willing to live in an area the higher the demand for housing and industrial buildings. Higher demand will significantly boost the price of real estate in an area.

Farm Rental

Many real estate investors are into purchasing agricultural lands and renting them out to farmers who don't have the capacity to buy the land or the eligibility for a bank loan. This investment can be tricky as you need to find the right farmer and learn effective lease agreement. There is no generic business model for a farm rental as the strategy you need to use will largely depend on the status of the land and the needs of the farmer.

This business model is usually ideal for those who have the know-how in agriculture such as retiring farmers or those who have inherited farms but don't want to cultivate the land so they opt to just lease out. There are also government organizations, non-profit entities, and private companies who are also into this business model.

The common end users for farm rentals are farmers who are starting a new farm business, expanding their farm, or those who are relocating their business. Many of these end-users are starters who don't have the working capital to buy their own farm and purchase the required equipment.

In this real estate model, the land could be a currently cultivated farm or has been cultivated a long time ago but has been abandoned. However, there are also ideal lands that were never farmed but can be converted into an agricultural type. Just be sure to check the land use restrictions to know if the land is under conservation or has been zoned as agricultural.

If you are interested in this form of real estate investment, you need to understand that you may have to provide the infrastructure needed by farmers such as water supply, fencing, electricity, housing, greenhouses, barns, and access to roads. Your tenant may also require added infrastructure during the lease.

Lease Agreement

Basically, your lease agreement for a farm rental should specify the important details of the landlord and the tenant on top of the clear description of the land and the facilities you are leasing and how the agreement will be terminated. Be sure to clarify liability and other forms of insurance.

In this form of real estate business, you need to specifically include the prohibited farm practices, the process for future capital investments, and responsibility for the land and the structures built before and during the lease agreement.

Lease Types

The common type of lease for a farm rental is a yearly lease in which the lease is renewed every year, so it is a short-term agreement. Other forms of lease include multi-year lease, renewable lease, and lease with the right of first refusal. You need to decide whether you want a short-term lease or a long-term lease.

Short term lease is more appealing to starting farmers, but be wary because they can easily move their business to a new location with better infrastructure. Hence, you may need to deal with several starting farmers instead of a successful business in the long-term.

Take note that a farm rental business is highly variable. As a landowner, you need to consider the requirements of various farming activities and their impact on your land. Grazing animals or haying is considered as low cost and low impact farming. High cost and high impact farming such as corn or wheat require more investment and calls for more land security for the farmer.

Finding the Right Farmer

To find the right farmer for your agricultural investment, it is ideal to specifically point out what your land is offering, what you are expecting in return, and which terms are negotiable and non-negotiable.

You can reach out to nearby farmers looking to supplement their own land for grazing or growing new crops. You can also get in touch with farmers in surrounding areas who might be interested to relocate their business. A review or an application process before meeting the potential tenant can save you time.

The vetting process could be very informal but you should regard it as a serious interview. A basic conversation over the phone or in person is a traditional approach when you are recruiting farmers for low impact farming such as haying. You need to use a more formal process if you are looking for farmers for high impact farming or if you prefer a long-term lease.

You need to screen out the farmers who are not a good fit with your goals. In this way, you can also identify issues that you need to think about before meeting the prospective tenant. There is no need to complicate the application. Just make sure that it will be able to provide you with insight on the agricultural experience of the farmer, the farm activities that he is interested in doing on your land, the support they need, if they have a written business plan, and possibly some references.

How Much Can You Charge for Rent?

The lease will vary depending on the farming activities and the benefit to you as the owner of the land. You may agree on a 100% rental fee or you may arrange a lower rental fee then a share of the profits of the farm.

Car Park Business

Some say that investing in car parks is no longer a lucrative real estate investment mainly because of the increase in research and investment to initiatives such as self-driving cars and the growth of car sharing economy. On the other hand, major cities are now trying to solve air and noise pollution by reducing the number of cars allowed.

However, buying a vacant land and transforming it into a car park will continue to become a lucrative business in the next 15 to 20 years. In spite of the technological advancements with self-driving cars, the growth of the car industry will not be significantly disrupted. These innovations will continue to gain traction but not at the speed that we expect. There are also challenges when it comes to regulation, which is the main reason why there is still demand for spaces where people can safely park their personal vehicles.

The Ideal Land for a Car Park

Location is crucial when you are starting a car park business. There are things you need to consider such as:

- **Convenience** - Is the location accessible for people to park their cars?
- **Zoning limits** - Does the city allow you to convert the land into a car park?
- **Traffic** - Are there enough cars in the area to make the business lucrative? Lands that are near convention centers, airports or shopping complexes are usually ideal places to look
- **Area Demand** - How much parking space does the area require? You may try talking to people in the area about parking, and check if your local government has available research for parking requirements
- **Land Price** - Check if you can afford to purchase the lot and then convert it into a car park

In looking for a location, don't filter out land with abandoned buildings. Take note that the location is more important than looking for empty lots. A perfect site could have abandoned structures, although you may need to add the cost of demolishing the building to your startup expenses.

Pavement Expenses

An important requirement for a car park is to have a smooth asphalt pavement. You can save a lot of time and money if you hire skilled professionals to do the job. Basically, the bigger your land is, the lower the price per square foot of developing it. For instance, a 50,000 sq. ft. parking area may cost around $1.50 to $2.00 per sq. ft. Take note that this is just an estimate.

Also, check with your local government office on the standards for constructing a parking lot. You need to follow the local rules so you can be granted a construction permit. Usually, you will be required to provide a drainage plan so the rain will not flow off the lot and flood the surrounding areas.

Nitty Gritty

There are three primary ways to design the entrance to your parking lot. First, you may choose a car park with no gate, in which you can trust your patrons to pay based on how long they park their vehicles. Second, you can have a gated car park that requires you to hire a cashier who will collect the parking fee. Third, an electronic gate equipped with an automated payment system.

The first option is most affordable but it carries the risk of people abusing the system. Hiring personnel to collect rent will cost you more over time compared to installing an automated system. But take note that an actual person will provide your business with the flexibility because machines cannot resolve complaints.

You may also need to consider if you like your customers to pay on the go or set up a membership service where they can pay each month so they can get a guaranteed parking space. You can choose one system or follow a hybrid model.

Security

Aside from the personnel who will collect the parking fee, you also need to consider the cost of the security and maintenance of the car park. If you want a big parking space that can accommodate hundreds of cars, you may add a valet service. This will add more to your operational expenses.

Security personnel are also crucial to make your space safe. You may also need to install a Closed Circuit TV (CCTV) and enough lighting that will discourage attackers and thieves.

Pros and Cons of Investing in Land

As you should know by now, there are many opportunities you can explore when you purchase a vacant lot. However, you should always do your due diligence whenever you are considering a business opportunity, especially when it comes to land investments. Below you will find the pros and cons of investing in land.

One of the main advantages of purchasing vacant land is that you have the freedom to create the property that you like. While this may require foresight, as you have to determine what is the best use for the property will be in a specific area, it provides you with a great window to be creative. Certainly, you need to consider various zoning restrictions, so you should comply with the rules.

Vacant land is a lot easier to remotely manage compared to rental properties. With vacant land, you don't have to concern yourself with electricity, plumbing, security and other concerns.

Investing in vacant land is a lot cheaper as a long-term real estate investment. Basically, the property fees and taxes are usually lower compared to a developed lot. Moreover, sellers of vacant lots are normally more willing to dispose of the property, so you could gain a lower price. You can even be eligible for financing. Its affordability could become your competitive advantage in the real estate game.

For example, when you buy the vacant lot for your second home, the value of the land may increase between when you purchased it and when you are developing it. You can use the land as collateral for a construction loan, which you can use to convert to a conventional mortgage without the need to refinance. Upon the completion of the project, the total cost for the land and the development is much lower compared to the retail value of the property.

Because vacant lots are a lot cheaper, you can even buy them with cash. This will enable you to have direct or full ownership. Owning the land directly can provide you peace of mind, especially because this is a tangible asset that will not depreciate. In the process, you can get rid of additional cost such as loan origination fees and mortgage interest that are usually charged by the bank.

There are also potential downsides to consider if you want to invest in vacant land. For one, you will not realize income right away. While you will not have any mortgage to pay, you will also need to pay other expenses such as association fees, the cost of improving the property, and property taxes.

Without rental income, you have to be creative so you can cover the expenses. Aside from renting out the land to farmers or converting the lot to a car park, you can also sell parts of the lot for rights such as gaming or mineral. You may also find another use (short-term) for the lot while you are still looking for a buyer or waiting for the value to increase.

It can be a challenge to secure bank financing to buy a vacant lot. Hence, if you develop it and then you can't sell it right away, your investment will be idle while you are waiting for your strategy to become successful.

There are instances that the lot can have physical issues. Many real estate investors caution purchasing flat lands mainly because of water runoff issues. Similarly, if you are looking into mountainous terrain, you may find it difficult to build properties. You also need to be clear on the situation with road access, water source, and sewer quality.

While you can still depreciate specific improvements like a new sewer system or roads, a vacant lot will leave you without any structure that is subject to depreciation. There is also no mortgage that is tied to a structure so you will not be eligible for deduction on mortgage interest.

There are required permits and approvals when you invest in land. The local zoning can determine what you can do with your vacant lot. In addition, the timetable for your project approved by local regulating bodies may also vary. You also need to check how many lots you are allowed to develop. This dictates how much you can make in this investment. In this real estate business strategy, you may need to add contingencies to your plan, which also includes your permit approvals. Do not buy the land if you are not able to acquire the approvals for what you are trying to build.

Scoring Land

A. Liquidity

Investing in a vacant land is basically regarded as high risk because it has higher liquidity risk. This means that a vacant land may take time to be purchased or sold in the market. If you want to sell a vacant land quickly, you may need to lower down the price. Take note that in a real estate investment, it is ideal to consider those properties that you can easily convert into cash at a reasonable cost, at a reasonable price, and at a reasonable period of time.

Just a few years ago, real estate is generally considered as a liquid asset, but this is not much the case today. The lack of liquidity for vacant lots is aggravated by the situation wherein very few real estate investors are comfortable in investing in vacant land. Hence, the potential market for investors is not that active. But with such risk, you can also expect higher returns. You just need to be comfortable with the risks.

B. Scalability

A real estate business involving raw land is difficult to scale as you can't just buy a vacant land and convert it overnight. This is in high contrast with REITs, which are very scalable because you can just buy more shares in a matter of hours. Purchasing raw land is a lot harder because you need to first do your due diligence, get the necessary permits and approvals, develop the property, and do other laborious steps before you can scale up the business.

2/10

C. Potential Return On Investment

In exchange for the high risk, the potential earnings you can gain from raw land investing can be substantial. This is possible if you know the strategy such as the buy and hold. For example, you can purchase a vacant lot today for a lower price, then walk away with the original price increasing to a hundred fold 20 years later. And while waiting for capital appreciation, you can choose to lease the land to a farmer as discussed earlier or convert it into a car park so you can start earning regular income.

7/10

D. Passivity

Once you have already converted the vacant land into a business that can provide you with regular stream of income, it becomes easy for you to earn money without directly exchanging your time for it. However, you still need to take care of the needs of your tenants or make sure that the car park is properly maintained. You can easily solve this by hiring a property manager so you can free yourself from the responsibilities of operating the business every day.

6/10

E. Simplicity

Investing in a vacant land is a bit harder than it looks. While the business model seems simple, entry to this investment should not be taken lightly. You need to do your due diligence first before you purchase any land to make sure that it is aligned with your goals. You also need to gain a lot of capital and study the market well to ensure your investment has the potential to be profitable.

4/10

Ten Tips for Successfully Investing in Land

1. **Have a plan** - Before you buy a vacant land, you should first figure out precisely how you want to use the property. Careful planning can help you choose the lot that is right for your real estate investment goal.

For example, land purchased for farming would require accessible water and roads to market. Moreover, you need to consider at what point you can call your investment a success.

2. **Understand the downsides** - While investing in vacant land can be profitable, there can also be disadvantages. Land is not subject to depreciation, and there are several tax advantages that are associated with it.

But, this form of real estate investment is considered as illiquid and ideal for long-term. Even if you start developing it days after your purchase, it may take several years before you can gain ROI. Selling it immediately is often not an option.

3. **Understand the factors that affect the land's value** - It is often hard to determine value although there are specific factors that can affect it. For instance, a land that is sloped could make development difficult and expensive. Hence, be sure that you review the depth, width, shape, and exact size of the property that you want to consider.

Location is an important factor. The prime candidates for development are usually corner lots with easy access to parking and roads. Other factors to consider are access to telephone service, electricity, natural gas, drinking water, and sewers.

4. **Be ready to face possible problems** - Look beyond the aesthetics of your vacant land. An abandoned lot could be even profitable than a sunny meadow. You need to check for hidden problems such as old septic tanks, buried toxic wastes, sinister history, and more.

And even though you may not see rocks on the ground that you need to get rid of, you should also check if there are huge boulders buried in the ground. This will significantly limit your plan for developing the land.

5. **Consider the environment** - Regardless of how you want to develop your vacant land, you need to know if it has the minimal necessities and the environment is pleasing. A flood-prone area can heavily damage your potential car park business. A nearby subdivision may impede your plan to rent out the land for farming.

6. **Know the total cost of your purchase** - Remember, the cost of purchasing the vacant land is not the same as the price you pay, because the sales price is just a portion of the cost. You need to consider the yield or what you can gain from the land once you developed it. This will demand more capital outlays for soil tests, engineering services, permits, fees, surveys, and more.

7. **Do your due diligence -** It is always ideal to do your research and uncover more information about the raw land that you want to purchase. Secure a survey of the parcel and personally locate fence lines, trails, streams, or ponds. Capture photos and look for the boundaries of the lot. Make certain to look for any signs of toxic wastes that can drastically lower down the price of the property. A closer look at the vacant land is well worth it. The more research, the fewer surprises you need to manage later.

8. **Love the land** - Before buying the land, be sure that you follow your gut and you are positive about it. You can ask the current owner of the land about the property and his reason for selling. Be sure to ask about financing options and taxes. You should also visit the neighbors and ask about the property and what they want about the area.

9. **Trust the experts** - Buying a vacant land is an extensive process, which can be easier if you have a team of experts to help in facilitating the sale. Ideally, you need to seek assistance from a real estate agent, a realtor, and a real estate attorney to iron out all problems before you buy the property.

10. **Know your timetable** - Time is an important element in developing a vacant land. You should consider uncontrollable factors such as the economy or the changing demographics in the area.

Interesting Fact #6

Monopoly was originally designed to teach players about the broken nature of capitalism. It's inventor, Elizabeth Magie, would have sent herself straight to jail if she'd lived to know just how influential today's twisted version of her game turned out to be!

Chapter 6

Industrial Real Estate

The thriving real estate industry doesn't just revolve around residential and commercial properties. The management of industrial properties has significant contribution as well. However, some starters and small-time investors tend to disregard industrial real estate because it seems not as glamorous as its residential and commercial counterparts. (Think of condominiums, hotels, resorts and malls.) There's also a misconception that only institutional investors can afford to put capital on it.

Industrial properties are sometimes deemed as a form of commercial real estate. It's regarded as the biggest; other types of commercial property include office and retail. Due to its market size, industrial real estate is treated as a category on its own.

Overview of Business Model

Industrial real estate is a key aspect of the global supply chain. It covers properties such as warehouses and factories. An industrial property is intended to be a place for making or storing goods. Some properties are flexible enough to be used for displaying and selling supplies. Others are even utilized for events, car washes, art exhibits, data hosting centers, and TV and movie productions.

Unlike residential and commercial properties, there's no alternative to industrial properties. If buying or constructing a house is too costly, prospects may rent or live with loved ones for a while. As for offices, users may be allowed to work from home. With the rise of e-commerce, some brick-and-mortars may close. But when it comes to factories and warehouses, manufacturers, wholesalers and suppliers have to make or rent industrial properties.

The demand makes industrial real estate as an ideal investment option. You can invest by being a stockholder or limited partner of an entity that manages such properties. Another option is to become the property manager. You may either buy or develop industrial properties. After buying or developing, you can lease or sell the property.

Types of Industrial Properties

Industrial properties are generally classified into three: factories, warehouses and flexible centers. The property type determines the kinds of potential tenants or buyers. Compared to factories, the demand for warehouses and flex centers is greater. However, factories lead in terms of quality of tenants.

Factories are built with production in mind. Thus, they are roomy enough to accommodate big machineries or a fleet of equipment. Aside from that, they have spacious driveway and parking area near its main doorway. These speed up getting truckloads of raw materials and shipping processed goods afterwards.

Manufacturers are the top seekers of factories. Those that are planning to expand their operations sooner look for properties to rent instead of constructing a new one. They usually go for long-term lease. Additionally, landlords don't usually deal with property maintenance because doing so might affect the production of goods. The tenants will handle property maintenance, along with monthly operational expenses.

Warehouses are made for storage of various things. They can accommodate shipping containers, big boxes, and vehicles. They can also serve as temporary storage place for production machinery while the factory is still being constructed. Individuals, manufacturers, suppliers, wholesalers, e-commerce sites operators and even some government institutions may rent a warehouse.

Flex buildings can be used for either warehousing or light manufacturing. They can also be utilized as car washes, show rooms and filming location, among others.

Depending on their building specifications, industrial properties could also be categorized as standalone, strata title, distribution centers and industrial parks. A standalone building is made up of one unit while strata title is composed of two or more units. An industrial park is an area in a city that are designated and developed for the industrial sector's use. A distribution center is intended to house shipments of goods that will be delivered to retailers.

Building specifications and zoning regulations prevent owners from changing the use of their industrial property frequently. In the US, zoning categories are referred to as industrial 1 and industrial 2. Industrial 1 covers real estate used in toxic manufacturing. Each town or city may also have a list of other areas that fall under the said category. In contrast, industrial 2 focuses more on warehousing and light manufacturing. When it comes to compliance and paperwork, going for industrial 2 is easier than opting for industrial 1.

Factors that Improve Industrial Real Estate Market

The recession hurt the industrial real estate market in the past. However, government intervention, economic improvements and technological advancements drove the market to stability.

Advancements in robotics and 3D printing are among the noteworthy factors that are helping the industrial real estate market, albeit indirectly. It's no secret that small to big companies outsource services outside the US for cheap labor. This prompted the closure of many factories.

In recent years though, there has been an increasing demand to keep all aspects of production in the country. Quality control issues, political rifts, high shipping costs, and extensive waiting period contributed to the demand for total on-shore production. The increasing affordability and flexibility of tech advancements help manufacturers meet such need. But due to the closure of many industrial properties before, someone has to make new ones to accommodate the growing on-shore productions.

The expansion of the Panama Canal is also beneficial to the country's logistics. The ports in the west coast have been carrying much of the US shipping trade for years. As the Panama Canal widens, more ships can deliver on ports in the east coast. This entails increase in truckloads of raw materials and finished products shipped to more parts of the country.

To help keep running costs low, manufacturers have their factories near ports. The closeness of their factories reduces waiting period and fuel costs. Because of the demand to be so near to ports, the market value of the properties increased. This is a boon for those that already have buildings in the area. However, beginner investors and tenants will find it hard to meet the needed capital to invest, buy or rent such properties.

With the accessibility of more products on the other side of the country, there will be more undeveloped lands where industrial properties can be constructed. The number of existing industrial properties is also lower than those near ports in the west coast. Small competition entails more affordable properties.

The rise of e-commerce came with advantages and disadvantages as well. The increase in online shopping activities makes many brick-and-mortar stores obsolete. This, in turn, lowers the demand for distribution centers. However, delivery of goods won't be efficient without fulfillment centers.

Every major manufacturer owns or rents distribution centers. These are the initial destination points of big boxes or wholesale products before they get shipped to retailers.

But in the field of e-commerce, middlemen like wholesalers and retailers may no longer be necessary. Consumers can just buy directly from the manufacturer through the latter's website or through an e-commerce site. Fulfillment centers make this possible. You can learn more about this whole process in the book: Dropshipping: Discover how to make money online, build sustainable streams of passive income and gain financial freedom using the Dropshipping e-commerce business model

The increasing need for fulfillment centers is one of the advantages that resulted from e-commerce's growth. Fulfillment centers are similar to warehouses in terms of function. However, they also play a role in ensuring quick delivery of goods. Recent studies suggest that majority of the US states enjoy delivery period of one to three days.

Right now, the use of drones in delivery is being explored. This is expected to speed up delivery to few hours to one day. If this practice goes operational, e-commerce sites will need more fulfillment centers. Delivery drones will adversely affect trucking businesses though.

Buying versus Building

If you want to make the most out of the industrial real estate market, buying or building will be your best choices. Your savings may not be enough to finance either option. To finance your purchase or construction, you may search for limited partners or take loans.

As mentioned previously, many industrial properties were closed down due to the various factors. These properties were built to withstand harsh weather conditions and minimal maintenance. It's not surprising that some of them are put on sale.

Such properties are cheaper than buying a relatively new property or building a new one. The problem with old industrial properties is that they don't meet the updated standards. They might fall under Class B building or lower. This classification will hurt your marketing and limit your potential tenants. The ROI from resale will be low as well. Even if you repair and upgrade the property, there won't be significant increase in the resale value.

If there's one redeeming quality about such buildings, it's their ideal locations. More often than not, they are near densely populated areas. Demolishing them and building a new industrial property in their place may be worth considering. But you need to weigh the time needed to complete the construction and the demand for the property.

The best way to get a Class A building is to build it from scratch. Building requires extensive research. You're going to study ideal locations, possible tenants, marketing strategies, and industry standards, among others. Moreover, it may be hard to find a contractor who focuses more on industrial real estate.

Despite the difficulties, the high ROI makes building a more ideal choice than buying and repairing an old property. It's also less expensive and less time-consuming than demolishing an obsolete property to construct a new one.

Planning and getting building permits may take weeks. Meanwhile, the construction period may range from several months to a year. If you add demolition in the process, it may mean an additional month. The biggest challenge with building from scratch is getting enough capital.

If you choose to build, you should know the **three key elements of industrial property: an office, a wide room and a sufficient parking space**. Even factories require some office space. It can be as small as 10% of the entire usable space. The wide room is for production or warehousing. As for your parking needs, make sure there's ample space for trucks and for the employees' cars.

The Most Important Factor to Consider

The marketability of industrial properties depends a lot on the location. Areas near ports and train stations are ideal in many cases. Densely populated areas are good locations as well. But this doesn't mean you can build any industrial property in these locations.

In the US, one of the ideal locations for industrial property is the San Francisco Bay Area. It's near ports. It's densely populated. However, the prices of properties are sky-high. Denver and Chicago are also among the good locations. For international trade, Shanghai and Tokyo are the top destinations in Asia, while Paris and Prague are representatives of Europe.

For densely populated areas, consider the age distribution of the members. If the majority of the population is 40 years old and below, fulfillment centers are more suitable in their locations. Such young population is more likely into online shopping than older ones. Thus, there'll be a high demand for fulfillment centers in them.

Factories are still best situated near ports or near the sources of raw materials. In industries such as food and drugs, many of the raw materials needed are time-sensitive. To avoid spoilage, they should be delivered and processed as soon as possible.

Industrial parks in top cities are naturally expensive. But to have an advantage over this competition, one option is to buy or set up an industrial property in the neighboring town or city.

Constructing industrial properties in less known towns may be helpful to the local economy. If there are many unemployed individuals in the area, you can help provide jobs. The initial cost of the property is also far lower than those in major cities. However, the marketability and resale value of the property won't be that good.

During the lean season, you can turn your warehouse or factory into a seasonal storage center. If your industrial property is located near bodies of water, storing boats during the winter season will be advantageous. You may also rent out your parking space if the property is located near event centers and tourist destinations.

Offering unique services can also improve your chances of getting high ROIs. In an industrial park where most properties are into warehousing, you might want to create a factory. Or, if the warehouses in the area are mostly for dry goods, consider cold storage buildings. This will be a hit in cities where there's shortage of locally grown produce.

You can also take advantage of the west coast's IT hubs. With some upgrades, your warehouse may serve as a data hosting center. Two of the upgrades you'll need are backup heating, ventilation and air conditioning (HVAC) system and reinforced flooring.

Despite having an ideal location, your management skills can either make or break your venture. The first step to better management is to know and understand the purpose of your industrial property. Moreover, keep in mind that industrial property can be obsolete in just a span of 15 years. Thus, your occupancy should be less than 15 years. You should resell the property afterwards.

Pros and Cons

It's an advantage for investors that the demand for industrial properties remains high. Year after year, the outlook for the industrial real estate market remains positive. The growth is even expected to be better than that of residential and commercial markets.

With subtle trade wars not easing anytime soon, manufacturers are expected to boost their on-shore production to meet the local demand. This will drive a greater need for manufacturing plants.

There's also the unending need for storage facilities, especially in countries like the US. A lot of people are materialistic as evident in the number of possessions they have that could no longer fit into their homes. Self-storage and storage containers are usually the go-to options for these homeowners. However, those who prefer lower storage costs tend to look for subdivided warehouses.

Tenants often go for long-term leases. Short-term leases come with higher risk of vacancies. Finding new tenants and re-cleaning your property can eat up your time. The re-leasing costs are higher as well. Re-leasing costs cover marketing, cleanup and repair expenses. Having long-term tenants greatly minimize such problems. But if you subdivide your industrial property or offer seasonal rental, you might not reap this advantage.

Tenants and buyers are also less picky. If you're looking for a home or for a commercial space, your personal preferences often come into play. Your emotions can make it hard for you to decide which one to choose. In contrast, tenants and buyers of industrial property approach their search with their business in minds. Their biggest considerations are usually the location, condition and facilities available at the property.

With less picky clients, you shouldn't stress about aesthetics in your industrial property. The things you should focus more on are security, accessibility, safety and durability. It also helps to emphasize flexibility.

Unlike prospective tenants and homebuyers, the clients of industrial real estate don't usually negotiate prices. If they see the property as a great asset due to its location and facilities, they won't mind the high rent.

You'll only have to deal with one tenant at a time. If you have an apartment or a commercial building, you're going to find and manage different tenants at once. It's time-consuming and stressful. With a rental industrial property, you just have to worry about one tenant as long as you don't turn it into subdivided rental spaces.

Industrial real estate properties can withstand months or even years with only minimal maintenance. Maintaining a warehouse requires specialty equipment and safety gear. The good thing about this is that it's not needed for months or even years.

The owner of an industrial property doesn't have to do maintenance when there's a tenant. This is especially true in cases where the tenants are into manufacturing, assembly or packaging. In these production processes, the tenants prefer to take care of the cleanup to prevent security and contamination problems.

There are fewer market fluctuations in the industrial real estate market compared to their residential and commercial counterparts. Economic and political issues can affect various industries. However, they won't cause outright closures and vacancies. They won't also influence the prices to go higher or lower in a span of hours. If you opt for annual payment of rent, market fluctuations won't bother you and your tenant.

The resale value of used industrial property is still great. Manufacturers, wholesalers, retailers or e-commerce companies don't usually buy a brand-new industrial property. They'll rent first and wait for used properties to become available. Used industrial properties are more affordable, but they remain suitable and safe for production and storage.

The bad thing about investing in industrial real estate property is that getting a long-term tenant isn't easy. Studying the recent business strategies of major manufacturers, wholesalers and e-commerce sites can help you in your quest for potential tenants. However, making a proposal will require much of your people skills. You have to be knowledgeable on the advantages and challenges associated with the location of your property.

Setting up an industrial real estate requires a lot of paperwork. To make your property more marketable, it should have building compliance certificates from leading organizations in numerous industries. It should also comply with local zoning laws.

The leasing agreement can entail a lot of work as well. Finalizing it may take several negotiations. For this process, always hire a lawyer to draft your leasing agreement and spot loopholes early on.

Compared to residential and commercial real estate, their industrial counterpart is at a higher risk of being the target of a corrupt government. Such government will make it harder for you to get the needed business licenses and certifications.

There's a binary vacancy risk. Like other wide real estate properties, you'll have to rent the entire industrial property to one tenant at a time. When that tenant doesn't want to extend the lease, you'll end up with a single yet significant vacancy.

Subdividing the spaces in your property can help resolve this problem. With subdivided storage space, you can allow individuals or small-scale entrepreneurs to store their things in your property. But doing so entails costs. Aside from buying the materials, you'll need to hire people who will install them. The management of multiple tenants can be an issue as well.

Environmentalists may question your venture. Environmentalists are never tolerant of industrial waste. Even if you're not the one using your industrial property for production, you may get dragged into the conversation because of your tenant's improper waste disposal. You can prevent this from happening by planning the waste disposal right from the start. Consult your contractor and the local authorities about the proper disposal. Furthermore, you have to make sure your tenant is compliant with environmental laws.

It's important to be as environmentally-friendly as possible. However, you shouldn't go as far as using green practices as part of your marketing strategies. It might backfire big time. Implement eco-friendly facilities such as energy-saving HVAC systems and glass panels. Glass panels allow more natural light into the industrial property. This can reduce your tenant's dependence on electricity for lighting.

Institutional investors and corporations impose risks to the stability of the industrial real estate market. Institutional investors are well-aware of the potential of the industrial real estate market. It's not surprising to know that they are increasing their investments year after year. Their contributions are a boon for tenants, but for starters and small-time investors, they are a hard-to-beat competition.

Many corporations also opt to set up their own facilities. They won't rent forever. You may offer to sell your property, but just like you, they might not want to deal with the costs and time required for demolition and construction of a new building.

With the aforementioned competitions, it might affect the stability of the industrial real estate market. Institutional investors can drive the prices high. Meanwhile, when manufacturers create their own facilities, it may reduce the demand for industrial properties.

Scoring Industrial Properties

A. Liquidity

It may take months before you can earn your first few dollars from your industrial property. Getting back your entire investment and paying all your loans may take years to happen. When managed right, the ROI will be high but you have to wait for years, especially if you put the property on a rental for a few years.

For many investors in industrial property, rental is their initial source of gains. However, a big chunk of the ROI will materialize once the property is sold. After the initial rent, the reselling period may take at least a few months up to a year.

B. Scalability

Physical assets like warehouses and factories are never easy to expand. You can't just use your parking space to widen your building. Buying the neighboring properties can resolve the issue of limited space. However, there are instances when this is just impractical.

In case your property is located in an industrial park, there's a great chance that other real estate investors in the area won't just give up their properties easily. If your current tenant has no plans of increasing production, storage or distribution in the area, offering additional space may not be worth it. The additional paperwork is discouraging as well.

4/10

C. Potential Return On Investment

The construction materials, industrial facilities and large-scale property require high capital investments. The good news is that the ROI can cover these expenses. Moreover, you won't have to worry about operational expenses such as repairs, replacements, security, maintenance, property taxes, property insurance, HVAC costs and utility costs. Your tenant will be the shouldering these.

9/10

C. Simplicity

Managing industrial real estate requires knowledge in building specifications and industry standards. Once you have handled this, though, the management part tends to be simpler because you'll only talk to one tenant at a time.

Having a contractor helps simplify the steps. But, there are costs involved. Hiring is still more cost-effective and time-saving though. It also spares you from the stresses of buying materials and subcontracting for other jobs.

6/10

D. Passivity

Once you're able to rent out your industrial real estate property, you can start earning passively. Before that though, you'll need to spend time, effort and money studying what property to set up, where to build it and how to market it.

If you want to capitalize on industrial real estate with minimal efforts, being a limited partner or stockholder will be your best options. However, you'll need to find a general partner or investment institution that's knowledgeable and well-connected in the field.

7/10

Ten Tips for Successfully Investing in Industrial Real Estate

1. Hire a contractor who specializes in industrial real estate. Building specifications and industry standards aren't the same with residential or commercial properties. It's only advisable to get help from someone who understands the terms and knows what's right for the venture.

2. Do a background check of the local government before buying a property and getting building permits. A committed government can see you as a potential driving force of economic growth. In contrast, a corrupt government can target you and your venture.

3. Screen your tenants thoroughly. Make sure your leasing agreement specifies what kind of goods the tenant is going to create or store in your industrial property.

4. Months before your tenant's rent ends, start negotiating for extensions. If you can't agree on new terms, plan for the upcoming vacancy by looking for possible buyers or tenants.

5. Apply value added strategies such as increasing doors, widening parking spaces, subdividing spaces and modernizing facilities. Modernization includes increase of CCTV cameras, motion sensors and glass panels.

6. Stick to properties under industrial 2. You and your tenant will face less environmental concerns than engaging in a property under industrial 1.

7. Maximize the cubic space of your property by increasing the floor-to-ceiling height. The ideal height ranges from 32 to 36 feet. Anything lower than that range is deemed obsolete and relegated to Class B building status.

8. Make sure there's a clause in your leasing agreement regarding the penalties in case your tenant fails to pay for a certain period.

9. To lessen your management duties, indicate in your leasing agreement that the tenant has to prepare and clean your property before and during occupancy.

10. The liability should be equitably distributed between you and your tenant. In case poor construction or the use of substandard materials caused injuries or damages, you should be held liable. If the accidents are related to the operations of your tenant, he or she should be responsible.

Interesting Fact #7

When Apple was building a new server in North Carolina, they paid one elderly couple $1.7 million for one acre of land. The couple had purchased the property 34 years earlier for $6,000.

Chapter 7

Commercial Real Estate

Commercial real estate refers to real properties built, developed, and used to generate profit. It is the umbrella term that includes industrial properties, office buildings, medical centers, hotels, farmlands, malls, skyscrapers, apartment buildings, and warehouses.

Real estate properties are considered "hard assets" or investments that have inherent value because they serve a basic need. Land can be thought of as a commodity in limited supply. The value goes higher the scarcer the land is. When the price of raw materials used to construct a building structure increases, the entire property becomes more valuable.

This makes investing in commercial real estate enticing. But what really makes it a worthwhile investment is that the value of real estate properties rises when the general price levels of goods and services rise. As such, they are used as a hedge against inflation.

The fact that commercial properties can preserve their value even during periods of high inflation makes investing in them even more desirable. They are a legitimate income-producing investment vehicle that not only pays dividends, but also serves as a protection against the potentially damaging effects of high inflation on investments.

There are two ways to make money in commercial real estate. The first is to lease the property and charge the tenants for the use of the property. The second is through the appreciation of the value of the property over time.

In the first case, investors earn a rental income for the lease of office buildings, warehouses, and skyscrapers. The lease agreements would vary depending on the type of property and tenants. Typically, an office building would have different types of companies as tenants. It could be a start-up company, a law firm, a publication, or a tech company. The company can opt for short-term or long-term lease depending on the need. Usually, companies opt for a five-year or a ten-year term lease.

In the second case, the potential income comes from the appreciation of the value of the commercial real estate being held by the investor over time. The increase in value is determined by the demand for the property or the area around the property. Strategic locations can demand higher rent and prospective buyers are willing to meet the price if they see the earning potential for their businesses or if it gives them prestige to boost their brands.

Another way to increase the value of the commercial property is for investors to take an active approach to add value to it. This means making cosmetic improvements, redesigning, and modernizing. This allows investors to charge higher rent prices for the increase in the property's intrinsic value. Any renovation made to the office building can boost the rental or selling price in the foreseeable future.

Pros and Cons

There is a lucrative earning potential to look for when you invest in commercial property. Commercial property rentals edge out residential rentals when it comes to the rate of annual return. Depending on the location, commercial properties have an annual return of 6% to 12%, which is significantly higher than the 1% to 4% of residential properties. With better returns, commercial properties are a worthwhile investment.

Another advantage of commercial property investing is economies of scale. This may not be obvious at first glance because of the significantly higher investment capital, but economies of scale in commercial real estate do exist. The acquisition cost and the operating expenses can be substantially lower on a per-square-foot basis, especially for larger properties.

The cost of large capital items like heating and cooling system wouldn't be as high if there are more tenants, compared to just one tenant in a residential property. With economies of scale, commercial property owners are able to reduce cost and increase profitability.

Investors in commercial properties can also take advantage of triple net leases.

Under a triple net lease agreement, the lessee will shoulder the real estate tax, the building insurance, and the maintenance expenses. The property owner will only have to pay the mortgage for the building. This kind of agreement is optimal for large businesses that want to maintain a certain look or brand prestige.

There's also flexibility in lease terms. Unlike residential real estate, commercial leases are not governed by numerous consumer protection laws that have stipulations on security deposit and termination.

To those who are short on cash, alternative financing arrangements are available. Evidently, a higher capital is needed to purchase a commercial property. Typically, lenders would require an investor to make a 25% to 30% down payment plus the closing costs. Many investors who had their start in residential investments may not be aware that many lenders offer an alternative financing arrangement that is more flexible and with less constraints.

This kind of arrangement is commonplace in commercial transactions than in residential deals. With this kind of flexibility, the investor's cash can be stretched a little more, which can yield a better cash-on-cash returns (i.e., better cash flow).

Evaluating the price of a commercial property is less "emotional" compared to residential property because there is transparency when it comes to the financial records of the current owner. Particularly, the income statement can be requested and from there, the price can be assessed using the figures. The rule of thumb is that the asking price should be within a threshold where the investor can earn the prevailing capitalization rate (cap rate) for an office building. This way, the potential return on investment can be calculated or estimated.

This investment instrument is quite rational as well. Investors can easily gauge more reliably if a commercial property has a high potential for success because the variables to which decisions can be made are grounded in rationality.

For example, the desirability of an office building or skyscraper is a function of its suite size, proximity to transit, accessibility, ease of loading and unloading, etc. The commercial property's viability hinges on certain variables that can easily be measured or determined.

Tenants and investors of commercial property generally have aligned interests. They both have a vested interest in upholding their good reputation, so they would go to great lengths to ensure that they maintain their business storefront or corporate offices. This is advantageous to the owner because the convergence of their interests makes maintaining and improving the property easier and less costly to do.

Tenants of office buildings and skyscrapers are typically corporations with a reputation to uphold. They have the financial means to pay long-term leases and they have their own property maintenance team to ensure that the property meets or exceeds the quality standards. This is one less problem that a property owner has to contend with.

The biggest disadvantage of investing in commercial real estate is the high initial investment requirement. A commercial property is evidently more expensive than a residential property that's why the barriers to entry are high. A single investor would have a difficult time securing financing and would most likely partner with other investors. Acquiring a commercial property requires a higher initial capital outlay and possibly more capital expenditures to address maintenance issues like fixing furnace and renovating.

A large commercial property with huge foot traffic from customers and visitors means there are more facilities to maintain or fix. When the expenditure is too large, it can eat up the investor's profits. The investor could only hope that the revenue would be high enough to cover the recurring costs to maintain a busy commercial property.

There's also increased competition as investors all look for the same things, whether they be the commercial property's desirability to potential clients or red flags that previous owners tend to hide in the most subtle of ways. Whatever the case, one investor would always be competing with other investors. Competition is high for commercial properties that meet investors' criteria. An investor must be able to have excellent negotiation skills or at least the business acumen to close the deal.

Investors need to express time commitment as well. Operating a commercial property like an office or retail building with more than five tenants can be challenging. It not only requires money, but it also demands time and energy. Dealing with multiple leases means that there are more potential issues to face on a daily basis. The element of uncertainty requires a proactive attitude towards certain issues such as maintenance, emergency response, and public safety.

Often, there is a need to contract professional services. A single investor may try to do things by himself to cut down on costs. This may be viable in residential properties, but it is not possible in commercial properties. Maintenance issues in a commercial property can be overwhelming for a "do-it-yourselfer". Emergency repairs are best left in the hands of professionals if an investor wants the property to be in tip-top shape. The odds that an investor is ill-prepared to handle maintenance issues are high.

So, at the onset, it is best to factor in the property management expenses when evaluating the price of a commercial investment property. Generally, a property management company charges 5% to 10% of the rent revenues to handle the job including the lease administration. This is something that needs to be considered when thinking of outsourcing certain responsibilities to a third-party.

One of the biggest disadvantages in commercial property investing is the risk of long vacancies, particularly when the market conditions turn sour and the economy is sluggish.

Additionally, commercial properties have more public visitors and there is the risk of them getting hurt or some people damaging the property. Also, these properties have parking lots where car accidents can occur. With a higher volume of people going in and out of the premises, there is always the risk of incidents occurring.

While accidents are beyond the property owner's control, a system must be put in place to mitigate the risks. Doing so entails additional costs that must be included when estimating the value of the commercial property. Risk-adverse individuals may find it difficult to handle such undertaking.

Scoring Commercial Properties

A. Liquidity

In any investment venture, liquidity is a crucial consideration. This truly matters especially when an investor wishes to exit the business or wants to convert physical assets to cash to pay off a debt. In general, real estate investments are non-liquid because of the difficulty to which the properties could be sold. It would take a significant amount of time to complete the process of selling, which includes finding an investor, negotiating, and closing the sale. Real estate properties cannot be easily converted to cash.

For commercial real estate property, specifically, office buildings and skyscrapers, liquidity is low because of the significantly higher price tag compared to residential real estate. As such, there are a limited number of potential buyers because only large firms have the financing capabilities to negotiate and close such a multi-million-dollar deal.

Skyscrapers such as the Trump International Hotel and Tower, Aon Center and One World Trade Center fall under the category of Institutional Grade Real Estate investment. Transactions under this investment type are handled by private equity firms, large pension funds, large insurance companies, Real Estate Investment Trusts (REITs), and syndicators, to name just a few. This means that the potential buyer should have huge financial resources to put up an investment.

The liquidity score would be slightly higher if the commercial property is highly sought after due to its location, brand, prestige, and other non-tangible positive attributes.

5/10

B. Scalability

Real estate investors usually start with residential properties by focusing on single family investments and gradually moving to duplexes, triplexes, and fourplexes. There comes a point when investors may feel the need to scale up and graduate from multifamily investment and move to other real estate investment vehicles to diversify their investment portfolios.

Investors would eventually set their eyes on the bigger prize and add a commercial property into the mix. There is a tendency to shift the investment focus when they feel that they have maximized their profits in the field of residential property.

The challenge lies in the financing of a commercial property. Although it is not impossible to own multiple properties under an investor's name, lenders might see this is as a red flag. The loan-to-value (LTV) ratio must be reasonably low for the investment portfolio to fund itself.

It would be highly unlikely for a single investor to finance a commercial property out of pocket, so the next option would be to find an investment partner with deeper pockets. Bringing in equity from other investors has its own set of issues that requires time and commitment to do due diligence.

Another thing to consider is that without a track record, the loan rate might be significantly higher, which eats up a portion of the profits.

Going the path of syndication is a form of crowdsourcing wherein a group of investors pool their resources to enable them to acquire properties that they could not afford as individuals. Without deeper pockets, the scalability for commercial real estate ranks low.

4/10

C. Potential Return On Investment

Commercial property investors look to the potential return on investment (ROI) as the key factor in making their investment decision. Achieving the desired ROI does not come easy. In fact, it comes with numerous risks. But if investors are able to identify the right opportunities, do their due diligence, and be comfortable with a certain degree of risk, then the ROI can be achieved.

If a high ROI compels investors to take the plunge into the competitive commercial real estate market, then it's important to look beyond the location, tenants, and lease terms, and think outside the common strategies. It is safe to say that the greater the risk, the greater the return.

The National Council of Real Estate Investment Fiduciaries (NCREIF) Property Index has reported that the average annual return in the commercial real estate sector over a 15-year period is 8.8%, which is higher by 200 basis points than the S&P 500 Index in the same time frame. In 2015, the annual return is 12.7%.

If an investor gets an ROI that is comparable to the sector average, or higher, then it's safe to say that the commercial property is performing well.

With a triple net lease in place, the lessee is solely responsible for the costs associated with the asset being leased on top of the rental fee. In this aspect, the investor is getting huge savings for the total upkeep cost of the property because the lion's share of the expenses is covered by the lessees.

There are complex factors that affect the ROI of a commercial property other than the operational expenses and some of them eat into the profit margin. Taxes associated with the commercial real estate rise when the assessed value of the property increases. So, the potential yield and the overall ROI will likely fall as well. The same effect can be expected with insurance premiums and interest rates.

Interest rate, in particular, has a significant effect on the cost of financing and cash flows. If interest rate is lowered, more funds flow into the investment, which, in turn, affects the demand and supply dynamics in the commercial real estate.

It is also worth noting that when the demand for commercial real estate skyrockets, the cost associated with acquiring a property also rises, which brings down the capital gain and total return. So, investors should be cautious about buying properties in a "hot market" because the market will eventually self-correct and prices will plummet. Rising interest rates usually trigger this correction.

In the commercial property sector, the ROI is tied largely to the rate of occupancy. If an investor can't get quality long-term tenants, the income is likely to suffer. Occupancy rates differ across cities and are affected by different factors including location, demand, and economic climate, among others. Under normal conditions, the commercial real estate is relatively stable and the ROI is favorable. This is why it remains a desirable investment.

9/10

D. Passivity

Most investors aim to generate passive income. It's essentially the "end goal" for commercial real estate investors. This is why many investors are moving away from single-family rentals and building a portfolio of passive commercial property investments. With a passive investment, there is more sustainable cash flow, considerably less risk, less reliance on direct oversight, and less expensive management cost.

The amount of capital required to become a direct owner or operator of a commercial real estate is too great for one investor. It is evidently a barrier to entry (albeit a good one as there is less competition!). To overcome such formidable deterrent, investors are opting to invest as a limited partner with commercial real estate operating companies. This way, they are co-investing with professionals who are experienced with dealing in sophisticated investment vehicles such as Real Estate Investment Trusts (REITs). Going this route diversifies the investment portfolio and opens the opportunity to choose different assets with less geographical and business limitations.

With REITs, investors looking to get a piece of the highly profitable commercial real estate pie can do so without actually having to purchase an expensive property and maintaining it like a landlord.

8/10

E. Simplicity

Getting started in commercial real estate investment is no walk in the park. Aside from the actual sale price of the property, there are other costs that will be incurred by the investor during the due diligence period. The cost will depend on the state or city the property is located as well as the size of the property. Some of the costs to consider before purchasing include the environmental report, property appraisal fee, survey fee, and loan origination and fee, among others.

Financing the commercial property is a formidable barrier to entry that not many investors can overcome. Office buildings, apartment buildings, skyscrapers, and industrial properties require deeper pockets and necessitate pooling of resources. This is why large commercial properties are owned by private equity companies, banks, pension funds, real estate investment groups and investment institutions.

Even after securing the funds either through bank loans or crowdsourcing, the investor has to make improvements in the property to be outfitted for the new business. Sometimes the property is still in great condition that only minor renovations are necessary. However, there are times when a major renovation and retrofit are required. More often than not, investors underestimate the costs because they make wrong estimates. These additional costs add to the already complex nature of commercial investment.

5/10

Ten Tips for Successfully Investing in Commercial Real Estate

1. **Master the fundamentals** - Owning a commercial real estate is the first step to achieving financial freedom. However, investors must be able to first understand, appreciate, and apply the basic financial and investment concepts. The reality is that not all commercial real estate investments are lucrative. A bad decision can lead to a bad investment which could drag investors under.

Mastering the basic financial concepts allows investors to separate the good investment from the bad, to maximize profits and minimize costs, and to add value to the property. The core of an investor's decision-making process lies in the accurate evaluation of the commercial property's financials.

2. **Set investment goals** - It goes without saying that goal-setting is necessary for any investment or business venture. It helps investors keep track of their progress. It also allows them to determine if they are on the path to achieving their investment goals. Goals must be specific, measurable, attainable, relevant, and timely. Setting lofty goals isn't intrinsically bad, but it can lead to big disappointment if they are not achieved.

Setting a goal makes investors identify what they expect to have in a certain time period and allows them to gauge their risk tolerance for investment. It is a practice in self-discovery in the context of investment inclinations. Listing down the specific goals and the course of action to take to achieve them can help avoid emotional investing, which is largely influenced by trends, speculations, and overhyped markets.

3. **Use data to explore the market** - The commercial real estate industry is so diverse that selecting a high-performing property investment can be challenging. Data matters when it comes to making a sound decision. Investors must know how to read and interpret the key statistics and figures, so they can compare properties based on a number of indicators such as price per square meter, rate of occupancy, annual return, and population growth to name just a few.

4. **Don't be afraid to look beyond metropolitan areas** - Prime commercial properties are mostly located in metropolitan areas. They command a higher price tag because they are more lucrative and they carry a certain level of prestige. Looking beyond one's own backyard can lead to more opportunities. There's nothing wrong with exploring and exploiting homefield advantage, but regional areas can be a haven for prime property investment.

Many investors fail to see that catchment population is big enough to sustain the business and the likelihood of closure is low. What's even more appealing is that it is likely isolated from competition. Well-situated businesses or properties can perform just as strongly as similar properties in the big cities, but they have the advantage of lower price tag, therefore, the yield is higher.

5. **Establish an exit strategy** - An exit strategy is crucial in investment, more so in commercial real estate. The absence of an exit strategy means gambling away the profits already earned and potentially wasting away future earnings. An escape plan must be developed before making the investment and it goes hand in hand with investment goals. This requires evaluating all options and weighing them against the goals.

Investors could opt to sell the property outright or hold on to it to passively create equity. The buy-and-hold strategy is appealing because properties increase in value and rental income can be sustained over time. Another option is seller financing, wherein interest income from loan is earned. The seller benefits from a monthly payment and a tax liability that is distributed over several years.

On the buyer side, it is an opportunity to legally acquire a commercial property if traditional financing channels refuse to lend. Another popular option is the 1031 tax-deferred exchange, wherein an investor can sell off his property without being required to pay capital gains taxes, provided that the equity is transferred to a property with a higher value.

6. **Find the right property** - The right property is the property that meets the investor's criteria. It can be an arduous process of finding as many prospective properties and narrowing down the list. Oftentimes, the key is building relationships with area brokers because they are the best source of information on properties, tenants, and business climate in the area. This makes analyzing the property easier because all the key indicators are locked in.

The choice of property must be carefully considered. What may seem to be a good choice can turn out to be a bust, and vice versa. Going against the grain can sometimes pay off big time. For example, many inventors ignore a property class (e.g. childcare centers or petrol stations) for simply being unpopular for a particular stretch of time, but they turn out to give above average returns. There is a certain degree of risk involved, but the investment can pay off.

7. **Look for alternative financing** - New investors may not be aware that they can seek for alternative financing if the traditional route is too constraining. Bank lending policies have become too cautious in the aftermath of the

financial crisis in 2008. As a result, alternative sources of funding are on the rise. Alternatives include bridge loans, mezzanine loans, and hard money.

Bridge loans are considered as interim loans provided to individuals or companies until they secure a permanent financing arrangement or an existing obligation is removed. Some entities used bridge loans to fund short-term construction while waiting for a long-term financing to be secured.

8. **Add value** - Investors can directly impact their property's value by taking steps to boost income and cut expenses. This requires creativity and due diligence on the part of the investor. Some examples of adding value to a property include improving utility efficiencies, creating new sources of revenue, repurposing and upgrading the property, making improvements in the quality and image of the property, employing marketing strategies to boost occupancy levels, and improving property management.

9. **Re-evaluate investment goals** - Investors enter the real estate business with a set of investment goals, but priorities change and new milestones in life happen. It is important to review investment goals periodically to ensure that they are still on track and relevant.

Big life milestones such as getting married, having a child, kids moving to college, or moving to a new city can have a great impact on investment goals. The same is true when personal tragedies happen like a death in the family, getting sick, or going through a divorce. Having the opportunity to review and re-evaluate investment goals allow investors to make mid-course corrections.

It is recommended to review investment goals annually so that adjustments can be made when necessary. Investors should also take into account the changes in the real estate landscape to ensure that the goals are still realistic and attainable.

10. **Allow for adaptation in the future** - In real estate investing, it is necessary to be flexible and adapt to the changing business landscape. Investors must be ready to shift gears and move with the times. At present, investors may be focusing on a certain commercial property class, but this could change several years down the line.

Investors must always be on the lookout for more lucrative investment opportunities while maintaining and improving existing property investments. Exercising some flexibility will allow the investment to survive and thrive in the future.

Interesting Fact #8

In a competition to build the tallest building, the architect of the Chrysler Building secretly built it with a 125 ft spire inside. When his competitor's building was completed, the spire was pushed up through the building making it taller by 119 feet.

Chapter 8

Retail Real Estate

Retail real estate is one of the most diverse and biggest areas of the commercial real estate market. Retail real estate properties offer potential solid returns for investors.

Types of Retail Real Estate Properties

A retail property is used to sell consumer products and services. These properties range from pop-up shops and individual stores to shopping malls. Retail stores include cafes, supermarkets, fashion stores, pharmacies, etc. Investors can choose to put their money in these types of retail real estate properties:

1. Malls

These real estate properties are easy to identify. These are commercial properties that house several retailers and service businesses under one roof. These are normally enclosed areas although some malls have outdoor components.

In general, the size of a mall starts at 400,000 sq. ft. The size limit is still unknown. The largest shopping mall thus far is New South China Mall in Dongguan, China, with a gross leasable area of 7.1 million sq. ft..

2. Factory Outlets

These are also referred to as outlet malls. These are not usually a building or an enclosed area. They're more like clusters of outlet stores of different brands. What's common among these stores is that they sell at lower prices than the department stores. Sometimes, there are food options available, but they are usually limited.

The size of factory outlets is usually between 50,000 sq. ft. and 400,000 sq. ft. However, some of them can go bigger.

3. Lifestyle Centers

These became popular in the 1990s. They are basically malls that have more open spaces and smaller buildings. These are smaller commercial hubs that are intended to cater to the upscale market. Compared to malls, the atmosphere in lifestyle centers is more relaxed and intimate.

The average area of a lifestyle center covers about 150,000 sq. ft. to 500,000 sq. ft., but there those that are spread out over a bigger area.

4. Community Centers

Community centers are often categorized as what people call a strip mall. Their size ranges from 125,000 sq. ft. to 400,000 sq. ft.

Most of these properties have a grocery store. They can also have huge specialty shops and a discounter. Community centers can also have convenience retailers like a drugstore.

5. Neighborhood Centers

These are similar to community centers, but they are smaller. Neighborhood centers are commonly called grocery-anchored properties. They also have convenience retailers. Their size can be up to 125,000 sq. ft.

6. Power Centers

These are properties where you can usually find big-box stores such as home improvement retailers or furniture shops. They also have large specialty chains and discounters.

Some examples of power centers include Best Buy, Walmart, Dick's Sporting Goods, and The Home Depot. The pad sites in the parking lots of these properties often have fast food chains and other diners. The size of a power center starts at 200,000 sq. ft.

7. Convenience Centers

These retail properties are small, usually only less than 30,000 sq. ft. They have convenience-based stores, such as drugstores, salons, and dry cleaners. You can also find other kinds of stores where customers want to have a quick service or purchase.

8. Other Types of Retail Properties.

There are several other types of retail properties that do not fit into the categories above. Some of these are:

- ❖ **Urban Retail Properties** – examples of these are the high-end shops along Manhattan's Fifth Avenue. They also include service shops and sales offices not necessarily located in a single building or complex. They are located right along the streets and are easily accessible to pedestrians. They usually do not have their own parking spaces.
- ❖ **Retail Stores in mixed-use properties** – these are shops and restaurants located in commercial or office buildings and multistory residential condominiums or apartments.
- ❖ **Tourist/Traveler Retail Properties** – these are retail properties that specifically cater to travelers and tourists. You normally see them in airports, entertainment hubs, and vacation spots.

The diverse selection of retail real estate properties gives you some flexibility in choosing where to put your money. The types of properties listed above vary in terms of investment requirement, income potential, and risks among others.

Pros and Cons

Generally, investing in the retail real estate market is a good long-term financial prospect. However, it is not something that you should get into carelessly. One wrong decision could jeopardize your income earning potential or even wipe out your money and leave you with nothing.

It is important to do a thorough research on the market. You also have to know the potential advantages and risks you might face. Furthermore, you need to have a complete understanding of the whole process of investing in retail real estate properties. This will guide you in making rational decisions while you work on closing deals.

Consider these in deciding if investing in retail real estate suits you:

The primary advantage of retail real estate investment is the high income potential. In the U.S., the average annual rental profit for residential real estate is 3% to 5%. This is considered to be beneficial. However, the annual gross rental profit for retail properties is much greater at anywhere from 9% to 12%.

Investors may also consider the potential of "turnover rents" that's unique to retail properties. This is an arrangement where the property owner takes a cut from the gross revenue of the tenant's business.

The longer lease terms also give investors an advantage. The average residential lease contract has a turnover of 6 to 12 months. A lease contract for a retail property is much longer. The average lease turnover is from 3 to 10 years.

This gives you a more stable 'basket' of tenant leases. Your property is also less likely to become unoccupied for long periods of time. Moreover, some tenants of retail properties invest money into the retail space. They usually customize their stores to fit their products and services.

Because of this, they tend to stay longer to ensure they get back what they invested. Giving your tenants some degree of freedom and flexibility in terms of customizing their retail space is an advantage. There is no additional expense on your part as the tenants would have to cover the cost of customizing the retail space from their own pocket.

Tenants are also likely to go for longer lease terms when you have a retail property that's in a high traffic location. This offers them a high level of visibility. Once their customers get used to doing business with them at your location, the business owners will not want to move their business elsewhere. Provided that there are no other issues and concerns with the property, they would renew their retail lease.

Investors in retail real estate enjoy limited hours of operations. The operating hours of shopping malls and retail stores are between 9 AM and 10 PM. Outside of this period, retail property owners are basically off the clock. On the other hand, residential property owners are expected to work any time of the day.

Bigger retail property investors usually hire property management companies. These companies take care of the day to day concerns of the retail tenants as well as any emergencies that could happen, particularly at nighttime.

Some retail properties also employ alarm companies. However, some tenants usually have their own people to handle such concerns.

Retail properties are usually less expensive than the average residential property. Because of this, you only have to pay a small capital amount in order to invest in a retail property.

For example, a small retail property can cost as little as $85,000. That is much cheaper than a small apartment that costs $200,000. The sooner you invest in a piece of retail real estate property, the sooner you will be able to reap financial gains from this segment of the real estate market.

Investors and tenants of retail properties have aligned interests. The tenants of a retail space are more likely to take care of the property than those who rent residential properties. The tenants/owners of retail stores know how important it is for them to keep their premises well-maintained. This affects their branding, customer satisfaction, and ultimately, business success. Both the investors and the tenants are working towards the same results.

As most retail leases are net leases, they require less in terms of maintenance work and costs. The tenant pays for most of the expenses that come with occupying your retail real estate property. These expenses include maintenance costs, property and personal accident insurance, and utility bills.

On the downside, economic conditions can drastically affect retail real estate. The real estate market and retail businesses prosper when the economy is strong. This means that commercial properties are highly in demand. In turn, the market value of retail properties will increase.

On the other hand, when the economy declines, the demand for these types of properties will drop. This is because the retail sector may be affected and business may fail. You may then experience a reverse in income.

As a retail property owner, be ready for possible long vacancy periods when the economy is down. To find tenants during difficult times, you can offer them incentives, such as reduced rents and internal fit-outs.

Before signing a lease, you must learn everything you can about your potential tenants. Find out how secure their business is. This will tell you how likely they are to succeed or fail and leave you when there is an economic downturn.

Changes in the area can affect the property. These include changes in the infrastructure of the surrounding area can increase the value of the property. It can also attract investments. However, there is also a possibility that these changes will swing the other way. Examples of these changes include traffic patterns, retail trends, and design.

This is why the location is crucial in retail real estate. The retail property has to be accessible, so it should have good public transport options and parking. Then, it should also have a lot of foot traffic. Lastly, the type of business has to fit the demographics in the area.

A retail shop can lose business if any of these changes occur. The value of the property can fall when the location becomes less desirable. You may also experience long vacancies.

It can be difficult to find tenants on certain conditions. It may seem like a simple task to find tenants, but this may not be the case for commercial properties. Retail spaces can acquire long-term lease contracts. However, it may be difficult to find a tenant who would commit to these contracts.

If this happens, you can have long vacancies on your property. During this period, you are liable for all the expenses related to it. This also includes the maintenance required to maintain the property.

There is often a need for quality professional assistance. Some retail property owners tend to be absentee investors. They are not hands-on in maintaining their real estate property. If you would like to do the same, you may need to get the services of a property management company. You have to be careful, however, in choosing a company to work with.

Do research on the property management group that you wish to hire. If you don't, you might miss out on important details that could cause bigger problems along the way. Make sure that you take time to evaluate everything before signing an agreement. You also have to check their progress every month.

Scoring Retail Properties

A. Liquidity

Selling a retail property is not easy. In fact, real estate in general is an illiquid asset because they are difficult to sell. They require higher capital to purchase.

It also takes long to sell retail properties. The process involves finding a buyer and completing the transaction process. Retail real estate is also limited to their location. They are affected by the changes on the local market.

There are still ways to sell your property fast. One way is through commercial property auctions. However, this has restrictions. Some of the disadvantages include uncertainty of a guaranteed sale and high auction fees. You can also give discounts to your buyer for a faster transaction.

3/10

B. Scalability

Scaling your retail real estate portfolio is important in achieving your investment goals. The first thing you have to do when scaling your portfolio is to assess your property. You can do this every quarter, but an in-depth assessment should be done every year.

There is a big chance that your retail property investment is doing well. This means it is giving you a steady stream of income. However, it will not be easy when it comes to scalability.

This is because scaling retail real estate involves buying more land. It also involves lots of other things, such as getting approval to build.

Just because you achieved success in your first investment does not mean you can simply invest in another retail property. Therefore, before scaling your retail real estate portfolio, you need to have a thorough research on the market once again.

You also have to do due diligence, so it is important to have a system. This system involves dealing with upcoming tenant vacancies, finding and evaluating property managers, etc.

3/10

C. Potential Return On Investment

Commercial real estate is the most lucrative sector of the real estate business. Among the types of commercial real estate, retail is one of the most profitable. Investing in retail properties is a great way to make profit, even for a novice investor.

Retail properties provide a stable income for investors. Tenants, such as government and businesses, lease spaces usually from three to 10 years or longer. As a retail property owner, you will have income security.

Retail real estate offers you higher ROI than residential real estate. If you want to invest in retail real estate, you need to learn how to determine the Net Operating Income (NOI).

NOI is the annual income generated by your property after you take into account all the earnings from operations. Then, you will deduct all expenses incurred from operations.

In retail real estate, NOI is usually positive because the operating income exceeds the operating expenses. The operating expenses include the costs of maintaining your retail property.

- Cleaning and Maintenance (CAM) – this fee is usually divided between the property owner and the tenant.
- Repairs – the property owner is often solely responsible for maintenance and repairs, unless it is specifically identified in the lease.
- Property taxes – some states tax businesses on their commercial property income. For federal taxes, you can deduct your expenses and pay tax based on your net profit.

In most situations, the property owner is responsible for the property taxes. However, in some cases, it can be stated in the lease agreement that the tenant will shoulder some of this expense.

Administrative costs – this is the payment for the property management company if you decide to hire one.

Property insurance – you pay for the insurance of the structure itself. Your tenant will pay for the commercial property insurance that covers the contents and other assets of their business.

8/10

D. Passivity

Passive income real estate is a great way to attain security in retirement. It will also help you have additional source of income and create a roadmap to attaining financial freedom.

If you do not want to take a more active role in your investment, then retail real estate is ideal for you. Retail real estate investing offers high passive income. Tenants can lease your retail properties with long-term contracts. This promises a more stable flow of income.

You do not have to invest much of your time managing your property. This is because you can hire a property manager to deal with everything, including maintenance, repairs, etc.

However, depending on the location of your property, retail tenants can be difficult to replace. They also tend to customize the retail space to their business needs.

9/10

E. Simplicity

While it offers greater cash flow than residential real estate, investing in retail real estate involves high initial costs. You also need to do a lot of research before proceeding and purchasing a retail property.

As an investor, you need to consider everything. This includes the location and the comparables in the area, which also include researching future development.

The comparables or "comps" are assets that refer to the prices paid for recently sold properties that are similar in style, location, and size. If you analyze comps, it will help you determine the market value of a property.

As a retail real estate investor, market research is important in the success of your business. The formulas on NOI, cap rate, and cash on cash can be confusing. However, if you master them, it will significantly boost your chances of success.

5/10

Ten Tips for Successfully Investing in Retail Real Estate

Like other industries that have a huge potential for success, you need to work hard in retail real estate investing in order to succeed. There are a lot of skills and information to learn.

The first requirement is for you to have a passion for retail real estate to excel in this business. You also have to learn all the methods you can use. Here are 10 proven tips on how to be successful in retail real estate.

1. **Get some training** - Learning as much as you can is the first thing you have to do. Professional organizations are available to teach you special skills you need to have for a commercial real estate business, including retail. They have courses that are required for you to be eligible for a real estate license.

Therefore, you have to look for a real estate course that you can take. You have options to do this at a physical location or enroll online. Then, you can work for acquiring a license to practice retail real estate. Your training will expose you to the following information:

General brokerage – this involves representing the sellers or buyers in real estate deals. The broker assists the client to sell or buy a retail property. They fill in for the client in meetings related to the real estate deals. Brokers are independent contractor. They are not employees of a real estate company. The compensation they receive is on commission terms. As real estate agents, they can deal in any type of commercial real estate. They also have an option to specialize in one type, such as retail commercial real estate.

Property management – in retail real estate business, you can also actively manage the day-to-day activities involved to maintain a retail property. Examples include contracting services, repairs, and maintenance.

The property manager receives a salary from the property owner for their managerial services.

Property development – this is the career path you can take when you want to invest in retail real estate. You will develop retail properties and lease them out to earn a profit.

As a retail real estate investor, you will arrange the financing and buy some land. You will then construct a commercial building for retail and rent it out to businesses. Property development is time-consuming and requires huge capital. However, it is financially rewarding.

2. **Organize your finances** - Buying a retail real estate property is not an easy task. Thus, you have to organize everything. More importantly, your finances should be in order before you even start your investment.

Your financial capability will determine the type of retail property you can purchase. If you go after a property that is not within your price range, the bank may decline you for financing.

To give you picture of what you can afford, you can consult with an accountant. He can also assist you in developing a budget. This includes any hidden costs that come with purchasing a retail property. He can also help you find tax benefits. This can be important to your financial state.

3. **Have a coach or a mentor** - In real estate, including the retail sector, you should avoid making mistakes as much as possible. Your business can grow much faster if your mistakes will not hold you back.

Having a mentor is the only way you can achieve that. This person is someone that you admire in the retail real estate business. You should be able to easily ask them for motivation and advice.

They should share their time with you while still making sure it also works for them. For example, you can accompany them during negotiations when they are closing deals.

This is a win-win situation for the both of you. Your mentor will be glad that they are able to impart their knowledge on you. They learn more by teaching. Then, you will also learn strategies about retail real estate investing. This will make you avoid mistakes that will waste your times.

4. **Create a solid plan of action** - It is always a good thing to have a plan when investing in retail real estate. Approaching real estate is the same as any business. You should have short-term and long-term goals.

If you have a solid plan of action, it will help you see the whole picture in retail real estate investing. You can also focus on your own goals. If you have a plan, it will make sure that you do not end up making hasty decisions. This is because your plan has all the actions you have to take to achieve your goals.

The retail real estate business demands your time and effort. Thus, having a plan will help you remain grounded. You can also get to focus on important matters.

5. **Work with a reliable company** - The name of the real estate company you work with is an instrumental factor in your success as a retail real estate investor. A reputable company provides their clients the security they need when investing in real estate.

Choose a company that has a good reputation in your city. This company may also have a good name in the state or national level. Therefore, you need to do some research about the real estate company you will work with. This will go a long way in boosting your chances of success.

6. **Choose your market wisely** - Like any type of commercial real estate, your market is important in retail real estate. Some areas are more profitable than others. For this reason, find one that has a huge potential for tenants and profit.

As a retail real estate investor, creating a successful career involves investing your money and time in the profitable areas. You should start by researching about your potential markets.

The market for retail real estate is usually better in the cities than in rural areas. This is because there is a higher demand for city properties. Furthermore, there are more business activities in the city and the properties command higher fees.

Try to enter city markets when investing in retail real estate. Also, make sure that you choose cities that have a strong market. Remember that some cities thrive more than the others.

Interestingly, real estate companies in thriving cities close deals and sign contracts on retail properties even before they are finished. The reason behind this is the high demand for retail spaces. Therefore, target an urban market or a city to succeed in retail real estate.

7. **Consider demographics and trends in the area** - When investing in retail real estate, you need to consider the demographics and the latest trends in the area. You can make smart investments by doing all of these. Moreover, you are also planning to have a secure future for yourself and for your interests.

If you have enough knowledge about the area, you can make informed decisions regarding your investment. So, to be successful in retail real estate, you should have a thorough understanding about the market you choose.

8. **Stay motivated** - Being motivated is one the characteristics you need to be successful in anything. You also need to be motivated in the retail real estate business. As you tackle the market, make sure that you find your motivation to work harder each day.

9. **Be patient** - In retail real estate, everything takes longer than investing in residential properties. It takes longer to find new tenants. Building or renovating a property is longer.

However, the leases are also longer. The key here is to be patient. It just takes longer, but the profit is higher than residential real estate.

10. **Select your tenants wisely** - The tenants on your retail property can either make or break your business. For this reason, you have to pick them wisely before closing the deal with them. First-come-first-served basis is not always the best option in choosing your tenants.

Interesting Fact #9

The designer of the Eiffel Tower, Gustav Eiffel, included a secret apartment at the top of the landmark that he could use whenever he needed to get away from the hustle and bustle of his daily life. This apartment is currently up for rent and a second one is being planned for the first floor of the tower.

Congratulations!

The sixth character of the password required to unlock the *Real Estate Business Scorecard* is letter z.

.

Chapter 9

Mixed Use

Another approach to earning a profitable income with real estate is to invest in mixed-use assets. While this is sometimes mistaken to exclusively refer to multi-story developments, a mixed-use asset actually goes beyond this description.

According to experts, these developments also focus on the integration and compatibility of property uses. These could also involve creating walkable communities that are supposed to ensure unhampered pedestrian connections.

You may choose to develop mixed-use assets in different ways. The primary requirement is that they should be an integral part of a place and be situated in locations with high densities.

You may develop them as neighborhood-based or site-specific projects. You may also incorporate them into redevelopment projects and smart growth initiatives both in rural and urban areas.

Overview of Business Model

The mixed-use business model makes use of real estate assets with meaningful components comprising of at least three revenue-producing uses in adjoining or similar structures. It combines commercial, residential, institutional, and entertainment uses.

You can develop mixed-use assets for a city block, a single building, or an entire community. These could be real estate projects by a government agency or a private developer.

An example of a mixed-use setting is a sky rise building with residential and retail spaces within. The area for residents is located at the upper portion while the retail spaces (that house fitness centers, medical clinics, hair salons, and other shared work spaces) occupy the lower half.

Historical Background

The preference for mixed-use developments is not a new idea. Ancient men have preferred mixed-use developments due to their practical nature. With multi-purpose structures, ancient men could conserve their resources. This is something that was difficult and maybe even impossible with single-purpose structures.

For example, they would build one structure that serves these three purposes:

1. An area where they can safely rest at night
2. An area for their day activities
3. An area where they can securely store their food

Building one structure instead of three saves building materials and occupies less space. Such a set up allowed them to be more efficient in the way they use space, move around, and perform their tasks.

Aside from practicality, mixed-use developments have the added appeal of being bigger and more interesting in terms of design. Through these developments, people were free to repurpose and redevelop their real estate assets.

People then had the freedom to decide if they want to operate multiple businesses in a single building with units that are mostly designated as residential areas. They could freely opt to add more commercial areas as they please or even incorporate entertainment centers inside residential buildings.

However, such arrangement was modified during the age of industrialism and introduction of the skyscraper in the late 1880s. From then on, laws and rules were written and applied for mixed-use development projects to regulate each structure's function.

Special Zoning Rights

The possibilities are exciting when it comes to developing mixed-use real estate assets. The owner and the investors are free to choose what types of establishments to have, the design of the structures, and the configuration or layout of the property units. However, their choices and plans will have to be in accordance with zoning rights for mixed-use assets.

In most countries, there are government and industry authorities who are tasked to draw up, implement, and enforce laws on property ownership and use. If you are not compliant with these laws, these authorities may revoke your permit to build and/or operate. You could be forced to terminate your project permanently.

The good thing is that most governments are in favor of having mixed use developments. Some regulators may even have incentives and relaxed rules for 'desirable' developers. This kind of environment is definitely an advantage for those who are interested in this type of real estate investment.

Specifically, here are the special zoning rights for mixed-use assets:

- Existing shopping malls are permitted to add adjacent offices and/or residential areas.
- Multi-story buildings with commercial areas on ground level and residential areas above are permitted to face main streets.
- Multi-story residential areas with civic and commercial uses can be developed in urban places.
- Multi-family residential areas can feature office buildings within.
- Neighborhood commercial zoning grants permission to convenience services in residential areas where these are normally prohibited.
- Office buildings that provide office-related convenience services can be developed.
- Parking structures can be erected.
- Shopping malls can feature detached (single-family) home districts.
- Suburban retail areas can be retrofitted to adapt a more aesthetically pleasing appearance and uses.
- The owners of residential areas can operate commercially. They can run small businesses in their building of residence.
- The owners of residential areas can use spaces in their building of residence for industrial agenda.

Built-In Diversification

Aside from their special zoning rights, mixed-use assets offer the advantage of diversification. This is great for those with significant investment in their real estate portfolio. It evens out their risks and offers great opportunities for more gains.

Mixed-use assets are already diversified in themselves. In one development, the investor enjoys several income streams coming from the different types of property occupants. You can have income from residential tenants as well as from commercial tenants in a mixed-use condominium building, for instance. When business is not doing good for your commercial spaces, you still have your residential units as your source of income.

A lifestyle complex, on the other hand, could give you even more sources of income. This, however, would require a lot more documentation and paper work. It would also be necessary for you to take a look at and comply with more regulations as the case may be. Specific use buildings would be governed by different laws and policies.

To demonstrate, here is an example of how mixed use assets can help control the impact of risk in your portfolio:

This example involves residential (1/3 of the asset) and commercial components (2/3 of the asset). If the residential component of a mixed-use property has sustained physical damages and fails to offer a decent return, an investor's income is still salvageable. The residential component may incur losses but the commercial components can gain high profits.

On the net, this investor ends up making a profit. The profits he was able to gain from the asset's components have compensated for the loss he suffered from the residential components.

Successful real estate investors diversify their portfolio with mixed-use assets and mitigate their risks. They are able to cover unexpected expenses and losses from one type of asset with gains from another asset type.

Pros and Cons

Mixed-use assets also have environmental advantages. They help reduce car and fuel usage, promote smart practices, and bring a positive impact to the environment. Some of the other advantages and disadvantages of mixed use real estate assets for both investors and tenants:

For investors:

They give more value to real estate investors. Because they can achieve better long-term returns, mixed-use assets are more favorable to real estate investors. These investors are willing to invest a larger amount of money due to the potential of a higher ROI.

With a lot of money allocated for their development, mixed-use buildings tend to be feature-rich and highly attractive. They are high-value properties that can help promote tourism and increase private investment.

Real estate investors incur lower infrastructure costs. Mixed-use assets are less expensive to develop compared to single-use assets. Since mixed-use assets allow the services for construction, design, and maintenance to be accomplished in one location, these services are delivered efficiently and cost-effectively.

If an investor wants to have residential units, fitness centers, and entertainment hubs, for instance, and he has to house all these in different properties, he would have separate infrastructure costs for each property. If they were housed in one mixed-use property, the costs would logically be lower for a single location development.

Mixed-use assets have better exposure. The more types of businesses in a single development, the more visibility it enjoys. Of course, these businesses have to be strategically positioned and marketed. Accessibility, security, and convenience are features that can easily make mixed-use properties more attractive both to investors and customers.

Mixed-use properties are easy to manage. Property management is more convenient with this type of real estate property. Everything is in one location and the property managers do not have to move from one place to another.

For tenants:

Tenants with active lifestyles are easily able to engage in the activities that they are interested in. Mixed-use properties often have several activity centers all in one location. Someone living in the development's residential units could easily walk to the gym, the pool, the library, or to the restaurant. They save energy, time, and money.

Likewise, these developments are accessible to public transportation so people living in or visiting the property can easily go to and from other locations.

Mixed-use real estate properties are healthier as these developments usually have enough open spaces for the tenants to enjoy. There are walkways, playgrounds, and hubs where tenants can have fun. The greenery also results in better air quality.

Tenants are likely to be more productive since everything is all in one place. Tenants do not waste a lot of time getting from one place to another. They do not have to commute far from their residence to their workspace and they can focus on their work and other important matters instead.

These living areas are great for extended families. Relatives do not have to live far from each other and get to see each other only during holidays and special occasions. They can live right next to each other in residential units in mixed-use properties. This set up allows them to preserve and strengthen family relations.

Business tenants will find mixed-use properties more practical. Businesses are closer to their customers when they are right where they live. Their employees can live right in the property as well, minimizing tardiness and absences in the workplace. The property is strategic for both the business and its customers.

However, despite the pros, mixed-use assets come with risks. They can offer challenging situations for real estate investors.

For investors, these properties can be difficult to market at first this is especially true when the area is still in the development stage. Not a lot of businesses and residents want to rent property in a place that is not thriving. The challenge for investors is to make their prospects realize the growth potential of the community.

The community might not always welcome the development as well. This happens when the development is seen to disrupt the life that the community has gotten used to.

Building a complex of tall structures in a mixed-use development, for instance, might not be a welcome change for a small quiet community. Some communities might also perceive the new development as a 'magnet' for heavy crime and traffic.

Among the issues that would make a mixed use property difficult to market are open and active resistance from the community, regulatory setbacks, and uncertainty in as far as the completion and delivery of the project.

Property managers who are used to managing single use properties might have a difficult time dealing with multiple types of establishments. While the need to hire several property managers specializing in each type of property might seem to be a good choice, it is not necessary to do so. It might take a little getting used to but it is not impossible.

There are tips and tricks that can be learned for managing multi use properties. The attitude of the property manager would be more important in acquiring the necessary skills to manage both residential and commercial spaces.

For tenants, a disadvantage lies in having too many people using the shared spaces. With the number of businesses and residents in one multi use property, it is expected that there will be a lot of users sharing the facilities and common areas.

Those who do not have rented parking space, for instance, could find it difficult to find a slot during times when there are a lot of people in the area. This could be managed by having dedicated parking spaces for residents and a separate area for visitors and customers.

Scoring Mixed Use Properties

A. Liquidity

If you want to get out of the business and cash out, you can't do it abruptly with these assets. Liquidating them might take you years and successfully transferring them to another's ownership usually requires a series of steps, proper documentation, and expenses.

A major factor that justifies the low rating is the fact that these assets come with multiple components. To put them out on the market, you would need to be on the lookout for mixed use property buyers as well as different types of buyers. This includes those who are on the hunt for commercial, residential, and industrial prospects. You cannot simply focus on just one type of buyer.

A redeeming factor that explains why this type of real estate asset did not receive a much lower rating is its value in real estate. If you find the right buyer, you can get great value for a mixed use property that's strategically located, built with excellent quality, and has great potential for growth.

3/10

B. Scalability

Just like how the rating based on liquidity is justified, a major factor that also justifies the low rating based on this criterion is the fact that there are multiple components that come with these assets.

Scaling mixed-use assets can be difficult because there are different types of property involved. Each type of property would have different business and regulatory requirements to alter or revise business wise or physically. You would have to worry about documentation, permits, zoning rights, and even community relations when you decide to scale your development up or down.

2/10

C. Potential Return On Investment

Mixed-use real estate assets have a high potential for growth and profitability. As an investor, you can look forward to higher ROI within a shorter period of time.

Despite the usually high overall operational costs of building, maintaining, and doing business with your mixed-use real estate property, you can still get a significant ROI. This is because the mixed income streams evens out your profitability. Whether or not a particular segment of your market is doing well, you are sure to reap benefits from other segments that are riding high.

It's another plus that this score on this criterion has already taken into consideration the investor's tax obligations for the ownership of these assets. Even with such expenses as property and income taxes, the ROI is still expected to be substantial.

9/10

D. Passivity

Once you succeed in building a mixed use setting and getting to full occupancy, you are assured of a steady income. The key is to have a sound marketing plan to attract both tenants and customers.

This potential to earn money passively is possible if you hire a skilled property manager. This professional will overlook the affairs in your building and supervise maintenance services.

An efficient maintenance services provider for mixed-use assets is important. Like any depreciable property, the income-earning potential of mixed-use property can dwindle over time if it is not managed properly. Conversely, you can increase its earning capacity when you improve the property prudently.

E. Simplicity

They can be a challenge to manage, although not impossible. They require expertise on multiple types of assets. The fact that they involve broad categories is a concern.

They are not ideal for novice developers because there is no "correct way" to work on them. Their purpose is to blend multiple land uses, which is up to your design to deliver. You shouldn't rush the development of these assets. A primary rule that you need to follow is to develop them so they can serve a vital part of their location.

Mixed-use assets are also not for developers with a tight budget. You need a large capital to acquire land and build the units, and enough funds during the ongoing development. Unfortunately, not a lot of financial companies and credit unions are open to the idea of funding the development of these assets. That is why most mixed-use developments are funded privately or through building authorities and redevelopment agencies.

The rating goes beyond average because mixed-use assets can be less challenging to get into for the experienced real estate developers. With expertise on the development of multiple types of property, it can be easy for them to dive into the field, work with flexibility, and succeed on the project.

They simply need to figure out a solid source of funding in the beginning. Once these developments are already built and occupied, getting conventional financing is easy.

6/10

Ten Tips for Successfully Investing in Mixed-Use Real Estate

Based on all the aforementioned information, you can conclude that developing mixed-use assets can be truly rewarding. It comes with a set of advantages and this outweighs the disadvantages.

Taking on the challenge of developing a mixed-use real estate property is not a walk in the park. However, its promising financial rewards make the hard work worthwhile. It would be a good idea to invest in mixed-use real estate development if you are willing to lay down the groundwork patiently and to have your investment tied up in the property until you achieve your ROI and establish a steady passive income stream.

Here are some tips that will help you succeed in mixed use real estate investing.

The Planning Stage

1. Establish a solid source of funding

The first tip for success in developing mixed-use assets is to secure your funding. This type of project is very costly. Unless you establish a solid (or unlimited, if possible) source of funding, you can find yourself stopping the development midway due to bankruptcy.

Even after calculating the initial costs for the development, you should be ready for all the possible expenses for its ongoing maintenance and operations. As you go through the construction process, some equipment may get damaged and you can run into manpower issues. These would result in unexpected expenses and setbacks. You need to factor these in when you draw up your financial plan.

2. Develop projects that respect their environment's heritage.

One of the top reasons why people succeed in the business of mixed use real estate investing is the fact that they are not completely oblivious to their project's neighborhood. It's a wise business move to commit to the preservation of the community's history and heritage.

The people in the community where you will develop your mixed-use real estate property should welcome you and perceive you as an ally rather than as an intruder. They should consider you as a corporate citizen who acknowledges their past and present and is committed to painting a better future for them.

An example of a successful development in this case is the prison that was turned into a mixed-use community in North Virginia. What once was merely a place of confinement has undergone progressive transformation. Old block cells are now loft-style apartments, a yoga studio, a fitness center, and a lounge room.

3. Develop mixed-use assets that are near public transportation.

Another tip is to leverage on public transportation. It's always good to be situated within easy access to the city's public transportation system. Even if you have a mixed-use property, your tenants would need to go to some other location. The customers of your business tenants would also most likely come from other places.

You need to make sure that customers are able to go to your property to do business with your tenants as they need to. Pay attention to the transportation network system and take note of the stations and terminals.

4. Establish good partnerships.

It has already been mentioned that investing in a mixed-use real estate development requires a lot of resources, not necessarily limited to financial. It would give you a lot of advantage to have other investors putting in more resources into the development.

Make sure that you partner with people who will share your vision and goals when it comes to the development. You need to want the same results and to agree on how you will achieve those results.

As the saying goes, "two heads are better than one." Having partners also means that you have people who will brainstorm with you and even argue with you as you find ways to gain maximum profitability from your investment.

Make sure that you partner with people you trust and respect. You need to be assured that you and your co-investors will be on the same page – even if you argue once in a while.

The Developing Stage

5. Focus on quality.

You need to ensure that the quality of your development will give you a competitive advantage. You cannot go half-baked on your investment. Otherwise, you are bound to spend even more or maybe even get into snags with the regulators and your customers themselves.

Invest in quality and make sure that your development more than meets the quality standards set by industry regulators and government agencies. The more that your property is perceived positively by your prospects, the more they will patronize you and the faster your asset's value will rise. The next tip is to focus on the quality of your mixed-use project. By ensuring quality, you have a competitive advantage.

If your project meets the standards in the real estate industry and comes with high quality, more and more people would want to check out what you have to offer. If they like what you have, they're likely to patronize you and your asset's value will rise.

6. Be willing to delegate responsibility.

There is no denying it. It takes a lot of work to build a mixed-use real estate business. When you attempt to do everything by yourself, you are bound to jeopardize quality and negatively affect your chances of success. You will end up with delayed outputs and you will get burnt out even before you are able to see any signs of returns flowing back into your pocket.

Just make sure to delegate the assignments to highly qualified people. Trust them to assist you and help you carry out your original plan. Among the professionals that you should consider hiring are property managers and financial advisers. You may also consult someone who specializes in mixed-use assets.

7. Stick to the plan.

Another tip is to be consistent and stick to your plan. You should always insist on seeing the bigger picture because it is how you'll receive high ROI. You might think that you need to rely on gut feel at times, but staying faithful to your business plan is always a good idea.

Stop second-guessing yourself every step of the way. For as long as you have exerted all your effort and exhausted your resources into drawing up a sound plan, you should trust that your plan is solid enough for you to rely on.

Assess risks and opportunities that you are likely to come face-to-face with as you develop your project and do business with your customers. Use the information to prepare your action plan so that you are ready with a response when these risks happen.

Finishing Up

8. Be more mindful of the quality of your tenants.

Even if you have the best buildings and the most promising business plans, you can lose out on your investment if you do not take care in choosing the kind of tenants who will occupy your units.

Just because a prospect has all the money to pay one year's rent in advance does not mean that he is a good tenant. He could be demanding and inconsiderate of other tenants and your own business.

Do business only with prospects with good intentions and have 'desirable' customer profiles. Remember that the quality of your tenants would also affect the way your business is patronized and perceived by your target customers.

9. Give importance to your tenants' concerns.

Establishing harmony among the tenants of your mixed-use property is important. This is why you need to have house rules for all areas of you property. Make sure everyone knows what's allowed and what's not.

Be open to comments, suggestions, and feedback. Check on your tenants every once in a while and find out how they're doing. Listen to their concerns and make sure that they are addressed accordingly as best you can.

10. Be up-to-date with trends.

Get updated really quick if you wish to be perceived as more attractive and appealing to your target market or prospects. The value and popularity of your business would definitely be much higher than if you do not ride the tide of trends.

Knowing what the trends are will allow you be more open to those who are looking to ride the tide of consumerism. A way to combat the market's unpredictable nature is to always know what's up in the real estate industry. You should be on the lookout for any new type of asset, as well as new approaches involving mixed-use developments and then address these concerns.

Interesting Fact #10

In California, buying real estate without water rights makes sewer and water hook-ups illegal.

Chapter 10

Residential Real Estate

Investing in residential real estate properties is a popular choice for the obvious reason that there will always be a demand for living spaces. There will always be a market for properties that provide the basic need for shelter. As such, you can also expect to be in competition with others who want to tap into this lucrative income source. You need a good business plan to successfully gain from residential real estate investing.

Processes Involved in Residential Real Estate Investing

There are basically three main processes involved in investing in residential real estate. The last process ultimately lets you decide on two possible outcomes for profit. Here's what you have to go through to earn from residential properties:

- **Purchase** – select and purchase a residential property. There are a lot of options for you and you have to be careful with where you put your money. You can go for traditional homes, practical apartments, or more modern condominium units.

  Spend some time doing research on the prices of properties as well as the possibilities and opportunities they present. Consider factors like location, population, and development in your evaluation of the properties you want to purchase.

- **Hold** – you would have to hold on to the property that you have purchased, at least for the meantime. This should allow you to set up your next steps. Your goal while you are holding on to your property is to boost your bottom line.

  This is the time for you to improve the property if necessary. You'll also be able to entertain potential buyers during this time as you already officially own the property. Depending on your goals and plans, you can hold on to a piece of property anywhere from a few weeks to several months.

- **Sell or Rent** – when you are ready, you can decide to either flip the residential property to get your investment back or rent it out for a steady stream of income. This decision would have to be based on what would give you the most profits. Consider current market conditions, consumer demand, and property trends.

Do these steps for each real estate property that you invest in. If you are planning on investing in more than just a handful of properties, you have to be systematic about your activities. You need to be sure that all your bases are covered and that you are able to factor in all the risks, rewards, and costs into your analysis. Be realistic in your estimates.

If you buy a property with the intent to sell, you should factor in manpower costs, taxes, and other expenses, plus your markup of course. You'll earn a significant profit with a piece of property that: you do not have to spend so much on to fix up, you can buy at way below market prices, and you can sell while the market is still hot.

You do not have to worry a lot if property values go down. You can draw up a plan to hold on to the property and wait for market prices to go back up again. In the meantime, think of ways to earn from the property while you wait. Renting it out on short term contracts would be a good option.

If you plan on renting out your property, you can look forward to regular monthly rental income. This can be allocated for expenses on the property like mortgage payments, maintenance costs, and taxes. To manage your risk, it would be best to choose your tenants carefully. You want to ensure that you will get paid and that your tenants will take care of your property.

Residential Real Estate Investment Strategies

You can choose from two strategies when you invest in residential real estate. You can either buy and hold or buy and flip. You can choose to concentrate on a single strategy or have a portfolio that combines both strategies.

1. Buy and Hold Strategy

When you choose this strategy, you take risks while you are holding on to the property. You've already put down your money on the property and you will have to wait until you recover your investment and gain earnings. Property values could go down and your property can deteriorate.

This strategy is best utilized when you are dealing with properties with long term prospects. You are banking on the expectation of being able to sell the property at higher prices at a later time. Or, you might also project a demand for rentals and plan to take advantage of the chance to charge higher rates.

With this strategy, you remain to be the owner of the property. Therefore, you will be responsible for payment financial obligations (mortgages, liens, utilities, taxes, etc.) on it. You will also have to take care of maintenance and repair needs.

If this is the only property you have, you have to ensure that your income on it is higher than your expenses. Earning rental income on a piece of property that you are holding on to is a good way to ensure that you have money to cover your regular expenses.

Whether you plan to rent out or re-sell the property in the future, you need to carefully choose the properties you invest in using this strategy. Locations where there is heavy competition are not ideal as you will not have much leeway in terms of rental rates or selling prices. There's a good chance that you will have to go lower in your pricing just to be competitive.

The buy and hold strategy is a good option for a portfolio of properties across different areas. This way, you even out your risk-reward potential.

2. Buy and Flip Strategy

This is a good strategy to make quick earnings on residential real estate. Flipping houses is fairly common these days especially with shows on mainstream television about it. These shows feature how properties can be bought, 'transformed,' and then sold at a much higher price.

In this strategy, you buy properties that are worn down or outdated but have a good potential for being renovated so they can be sold. These properties can be bought at really low prices. With the right improvements, you can quickly 'flip' these properties and sell them at thousands of dollars in profits.

Your calculations have to be spot-on when you use this strategy. You need to be able to estimate how much money you need to improve the property and jack up its price. You also need to accurately project how much you can sell the property for. Otherwise, you might end up selling the property for less than what you spent for repairs and renovations.

Note that flippers do not only look at the aesthetics of the properties they want to invest in. There are also 'hidden' flaws and damage that could make flipping expensive and jeopardize an investor's potential profits. Even if the properties are selling at rock bottom prices, a flipper still has to take steps to do a thorough inspection.

These strategies appeal to different types of investors. Your choice on which strategy to use depends on how much risk you want to take, what you are willing to do, and how soon you wish to reap gains among others.

Comparing Investment Strategies

It is recommended to compare the two real estate investment strategies first to evaluate which one is best for you. There are a lot of things to consider, but they are mostly about your own goals and resources as well as what you are comfortable with.

Here are some things for you to consider when you compare the two strategies:

1. The buy and hold strategy is a good way to set up a positive cash flow.

This is particularly true for rentals. While you are holding on to a piece of property until it appreciates in value, you can rent it out and collect regular income from your tenants. Once you are ready to sell, you can decide not to renew your rental agreement and put the property in the market.

2. The buy and flip strategy could be risky.

It's easy to get drawn to flipping because of its media exposure. When you plunge into this kind of undertaking without knowing exactly what you are supposed to do, you are exposing yourself to risks.

3. Upgrades do not always boost a property's value.

Flipping, therefore, is not always a good option. Not all rundown property has a good potential for being flipped. Before you put down your money on a property for flipping, thoroughly evaluate the work that needs to be done, the amount of money you need to spend, and the prospective selling price.

4. Both strategies entail costs as you retain ownership.

In the buy and hold strategy, you need to make sure that the property generates enough income to cover these costs. In a buy and flip strategy, you have to ensure that you impute these costs into your selling price.

5. The longer it takes for you to do your renovations, the more expensive it could be for you.

Costs can easily skyrocket when your renovations drag on. At the same time, the market could just as easily turn unfavorable for you. That's why you need a good plan when you decide to buy a piece of residential property for flipping.

6. Keep in mind that the market can easily change

So if you're left holding the property longer than you expected, you might be in it for a loss. In such a situation, you lose your advantage and may be turned into the type of seller that buyers can easily take advantage of.

7. Dealing with third-party suppliers and contractors

When you flip a property, you have to deal with third-party suppliers and contractors. Instead of acting as an investor, you can easily turn into a project manager. And if you're not up for the task, it can be quite a pain in the neck.

8. Pricing Correctly

Apart from mortgage payments and upgrades, you have to factor in man hours when you reprice the home for sale. Add to these taxes, fees, and other legal costs and you might not even break even. This is why you shouldn't just jump in when you see a home you'd think you'll make a buck on.

If you are looking for a solid real estate investment, you should always focus on realistic return figures that factor all elements in. Do not get blinded by the potential for huge returns. Consider what you need to do or spend to actually realize these gains.

The property that you buy should match the strategy that you want to use. If you are new to real estate investing, find a pro or mentor who can help you out especially with the calculations.

The Pros and Cons of Investing in Residential Real Estate

Weigh these pros and cons before you invest in real estate properties:

The Pros

A great thing about investing in residential real estate is that you have direct control over the properties you buy. Whether you decide to buy and hold, rent, upgrade, or flip, what happens to your property will be according to your own discretion. You have the freedom to decide on what you want to do.

Investing in residential real estate gives you several options to earn income. You can also determine how much income to make on a piece of property. The property becomes part of your assets and you can determine how you use it while it is within your ownership and control.

The Cons

Buying real estate property can eat away a large chunk of your money. You need to have cash to make such a hefty investment. Given that markets can be fickle and there are no guarantees of making profits whether from holding or from flipping, you'll be taking a huge risk here.

If you decide to secure funding for any property, expect it to be quite challenging if you don't have a regular line of credit with a bank or financial institution. Especially when it comes to pure investments like these, the lack of any guarantees may disqualify you from being granted an adequate amount of financing.

It takes more work than just putting down the money as an investor in order to profit from residential real estate. You'll have to be willing and able to put on other 'hats' too. You might have to act as a property manager, a contractor, or even an interior decorator in the process of making your investment more appealing to your potential clients.

If you decide to hold and rent, you may also experience problems with finding tenants. In some cases, you might even have to deal with vacancies. When your calculations allocate your rental income to paying for your monthly expenses and month obligations, vacancies can easily affect your monthly balance.

There are also legal concerns to be aware of when you invest in residential real estate properties. Laws differ depending on where the properties are located. In most cases, having professionals around to give you sound advice is necessary.

Scoring Residential Real Estate

A. Liquidity

With residential real estate, you are looking at anywhere from several months to years to dispose of properties at the right price. This also accounts for the time necessary to fix the properties up for flipping. This means that your money is tied up until you sell the property. Even if you decide to rent out the property, it is not likely for you to recover your principal investment in the near future.

Investing in residential real estate does not give you a lot of liquidity. If you need to recover your investment right away, you might want to think twice about putting it in this asset class. If you are not in a hurry, you can benefit from the high potential income residential real estate investing can give you.

3/10

B. Scalability

It is not easy to scale your residential real estate portfolio up or down. You cannot just decide to pare down your portfolio or expand it within a number of days or even weeks.

To add more properties to the mix, you'll need to have a lot of additional funding add to that spend hours searching and studying locations and available homes. In this case, considering that you're an average investor, it may not be the most scalable option there is.

3/10

C. Potential Return On Investment

Your potential ROI will depend on the market, demand, and your choice of location. But provided that you do things right and invest at a proper time, you can earn a lot from an investment in residential real estate whether you choose to go for a sale or decide to rent out your property.

Of course there will be certain fees that will affect your bottom line. There are taxes, permits, construction expenses, interest rates, mortgage payments, and additional expenses that you have to include in your final figures.

7/10

D. Passivity

Those who are looking for a passive income stream would have to choose the right strategy for their residential real estate portfolio. It is possible to set up a passive income stream from a portfolio of rental properties on long term contracts and lease agreements.

The buy and flip strategy might be intimidating for those who simply want to invest and then wait for steady returns on their money. This strategy also requires investors to be more hands-on and involved in the improvements that need to be done. Investors need to put in ample time and resources to profit from residential real estate investing.

6/10

E. Simplicity

It's easy enough to do business in residential real estate. You only need to have enough money to buy your first property. There really are no barriers to entry.

Even earning from your investment is simple enough since you can actually just buy and then sell the property outright as is. When you have had enough experience and learned the ropes, you can venture into more strategic residential real estate investing for long term yields.

The residential real estate market holds a lot of earning potential for every investor who is willing to put in the money, time, and effort. If these scores are aligned with your own investment objectives, knowledge, and risk appetite, then go ahead and look for worthwhile residential properties to earn income from.

8/10

Ten Tips for Successfully Investing in Residential Real Estate

Even if it is simple enough to get into residential real estate investing, you still have to put in your share of time and effort to be successful in it. As in any worthwhile investment, a combination of preparation, strategy, and good business sense are necessary. Here are 10 tips to help you succeed in this particular business endeavor:

1. Research about the properties you are interested in.

Due diligence can be a lifesaver when it comes to property investments. Do not take things at face value. Evaluate your options thoroughly to avoid wasting your money on duds and properties that could end up worth a lot less than what you bought them for.

Look into titles and liens. Check on past ownership and property history. Everything should be transparent and any risk that comes with the property should be clear to you. Weigh your options and make sure that any risk you will be taking on is worth the potential profit.

Do not hesitate to consult with professionals if you have doubts or if you need to clarify some issues before you move forward with your investment.

2. Invest in house inspections prior to purchasing any piece of property.

You might hesitate in incurring any costs before you even own the property, but it's an insignificant expense that could save you from more losses.

Through an inspection, you can spot issues that need to be addressed. You can demand to have these fixed first before you continue with your transaction or you can negotiate for a lower price because of these issues.

You may also decide that the issues discovered during the inspection are deal-breakers for you. In this case, you can go and look at other properties instead of wasting your time hovering over a piece of property that you are unsure of buying.

3. Make sure there isn't any serious structural damage in any property you are investing in.

Watch out for this if you are looking to flip properties. Rundown does not necessarily mean unsafe and inhabitable. Unless you are willing to rebuild the property from the ground up, it is best to stay away from properties that are not structurally sound anymore.

Wall gaps, uneven windows, and cracked floors are some of the signs that indicate possible structural damage. It is best to consult experts and engineers about these issues. You cannot just base your decisions on your own speculations.

4. Focus on minimal improvements first.

When looking for properties to flip, choose those that require minimal improvements or those that will not require a lot of money to fix up. Simple upgrades like a fresh coat of paint, updated hardware, and refurbished fixtures can already give you a lot of room to jack up your selling price.

5. Do not over-improve the property.

You might get carried away with your ideas for renovation. The temptation to turn whatever is in your imagination into reality might be too strong. Resist the urge to go all out in your improvements.

Focus your attention on making basic improvements and, as much as possible, leave your personal preferences out of it. Let the new homeowners worry about the major details and highlights. Buyers would appreciate having a 'blank slate' that they can paint on according to their own image of an ideal home.

6. Do the math and estimate your potential profits.

Take the time to make your calculations on what your costs are and how much you can expect to earn from your investment. It's not the same with all the properties that you buy. You have to consider variable costs for items like repairs and permits.

Add the costs to the selling price and compare it with the property's market value. Ideally, you should be able to sell the property at a price that covers your principal investment, the expenses you incurred to improve the property, and your markup. If the market values are below this price, it's not worth investing in the property unless you foresee a future time when it will be profitable.

7. Include miscellaneous costs in your budget.

Don't make the mistake of using up all your investment funds for buying a piece of property. Leave enough cash for repairs and other expenses necessary to boost the value of the property. Consider this as your 'operating' budget.

When you sell the property, you can include your operating costs in you selling price. You can do the same thing when you compute for your rental rates.

8. Work with a knowledgeable local realtor.

Make your property search easier by working with a local realtor. While you can look for properties to invest in on your own, a local realtor can point you in the right direction and show you the properties that fit your criteria. This way, you do not waste your time and energy scouring the market for great deals and profitable investment prospects.

9. Don't fall in love with any property.

It's all for profit. You are not investing in properties to have and to hold for your own personal use. Don't get too attached as it will be difficult for you to remain objective especially during negotiations. You might love the property strong enough to not want to sell it or let go of it anymore.

10. Be open to selling under market value.

Your goal for investing in residential real estate is to make profits, of course. There are times, however, when you need to take a loss. This happens in most investment instruments. You just have to be ready to cut your losses as soon as they become imminent.

It is possible for you to sell under market value and still profit from the transaction. This would put cash back into your investment budget so you can use it for more profitable undertakings.

Conclusion

Before anything else, I would like to thank you for reading this book up to this point. That only shows that you are truly serious in achieving success with real estate investing. Being serious about it is a good start. It also prepares you in developing the right mindset.

Furthermore, I want to share with you something that I find terribly sad. Once people start reading a book, they typically only read 10 percent of it before they give up or forget about it. Only 10 percent. What's sad about this is that from this statistic, we can see that very few people actually follow through on what they commit to (at least when it comes to reading). The reason for this is harsh but understandable: most people are not willing to hold themselves accountable. People "want" and "want" all day, but very few actually have the fortitude to put in the work.

So what's my point? First, I am trying to tell you that if you're reading these words, you are a statistical anomaly (and I am grateful for you). But here's the kicker: in order to become successful as a result of this book, you are going to have to be in the .1 percent. You need to take action.

Finally..

There is great potential for investment earnings and growth in the real estate market. The range of available real estate investments gives something for all types of investors. All of these have their pros and cons that any investor can successfully manage with the right preparation and strategy. Given time, money, and effort, you can put together a portfolio of real estate investments that will give you substantial gains both in the short term and over the long term.

You have publicly-traded investments known as REITs (Real Estate Investment Trust), company-owned properties via REIGs (Real Estate Investment Groups), and RELPs (Real Estate Limited Partnership). You can also invest in tax lien certificates, direct purchase of land or industrial properties, direct purchase of commercial and residential lots, as well as retail and mixed-used facilities.

Investing in real estate regardless of the type can be quite daunting indeed. To wrap things up, here are some final tips:

- Start by choosing a property type to invest in and research viable funding options. Take a look at your current credit score, investor relations, and of course taxes and other potential costs.
- Also make sure that you take a closer look into trends. How is the market doing? Which areas are best to invest in? Where do people desire to live? What types of facilities are people looking for these days? These are just some of the questions that you should be answering early on in the process.
- Learn as much as you can about the trade and all processes involved. If you have to work with an expert then do so. If you need to take a class or seminar then don't be afraid to sign up. The thing about real estate investing is that's it's a long-term endeavor and commitment so make sure it's an industry that you really want to get into before making that big leap.
- If borrowing money becomes an option, study your options and see where it's best to facilitate such a transaction. It is possible for your personal assets to become collaterals if you're not working under

corporate terms. Just make sure that you secure yourself before putting any payments down on a property.

Remember that no investment can give you substantial and sustainable gains overnight. You have to be willing to do some amount of work even to set up passive streams of income. Investing in the real estate market can only be worthwhile if you put in your share of work. Having read this book from beginning to end, I have no doubt you're the type that's willing to put in the work. With that, I wish you the very best of luck with your investments!

Part 2

Credit Card and Credit Repair Secrets

Discover How to Repair Your Credit

Get a 700+ Credit Score, Access Business Startup

Funding and Travel For Free Using

Reward Credit Cards

By

Michael Ezeanaka

www.MichaelEzeanaka.com

Additional Funding Sources Booklet

This current book will reveal 6 ways you can fund your new start-up business. However, there are a few others you can explore. How would you like to download a booklet that **explains step-by-step**, five (5) additional funding sources? If you want it, a PDF version of the card is hosted on my **website** and can be downloaded for free. However, a password is required to unlock the download. Follow the steps below to **retrieve the password**!

Steps to take

1. The password consists of 8 characters (all lower case)
2. Here is the incomplete password: q-p-d-k-
3. The **second**, **fourth**, **sixth** and **eighth** character of the password is missing and is located in random pages of this book.
4. **Read this book** carefully to locate and retrieve them (they're so obvious you can't miss them).
5. Once you have the complete password then go to www.MichaelEzeanaka.com > Free Stuff > Ebooks/Audiobooks > Additional Funding Sources, enter the password, download the booklet and enjoy!

Introduction

So many people do not fully understand the power of credit. It is a very potent weapon that has the power to do good or bad depending on how it's applied by the end user. In order to fully understand how credit works (so as to position yourself to take full advantage of it), one needs to grasp the fundamental concept of a credit score.

A credit score is not just a number. It could be your ticket to a quick loan approval, low interest rates, access to exclusive airport lounges, and even free plane rides.

On the other hand, institutions and individuals can also use those same numbers to reject your loan applications and give you unfavorable deals. Such will be the case if you have a bad credit score.

This book aims to help you achieve and maintain good credit rating whilst making you aware of all the perks that are potentially available to you as a credit user. While this DOES NOT contain guaranteed shortcuts to getting more money, it will provide you a better understanding of personal credit and how to get the most value out of the money you spend —a key aspect that brings you a step closer to financial independence.

Understanding your credit starts with learning how and why it was formed. The first chapter of this book will introduce you to the early uses of loans, types of credit, and development of credit reporting. Lending and credit reporting aren't as modern as you think.

Contrary to what you may feel about them, credit reports and scores aren't made to make your life difficult. Different entities take these into consideration to measure the risk of dealing with you. As for you, being mindful of your credit history and score can help instill self-discipline. You'll find out how these happen with the help of this book.

Furthermore, you'll learn more about the advantages of having good credit and disadvantages of getting a bad one. Maintaining a favorable credit requires being committed and attentive. Remind yourself of the pros and cons if you get too lazy to fix your credit score.

If you have a bad credit score, you should know that there's still hope. Some lenders may still approve your loan application. However, don't expect them to give you ideal interest rates.

The good news is that you don't have to settle with such deals. With the help of this book, **you'll discover plenty of ways of fixing your credit**. You may apply them first to boost your scores and win better interest rates afterwards. You should know though that repairing your credit can take a lot of time, effort and patience.

On rare occasions, it's hard for some people to get high credit score even if they're doing a lot to improve it and they're handling their finances well. Identity thieves could be blamed for this. **This book will show you how to protect yourself from such criminals.**

Credit reporting agencies weigh on different factors to determine your FICO scores and VantageScore. Get to know these factors with the help of this book.

The scores aren't as subjective as some people claim. Aside from the factors considered in computing credit scores, **this book will also show you the factors that aren't taken into account.** You have fewer things to worry about if you know precisely which factors don't really affect your credit. That way, you focus your attention on the factors that really matter.

Once you're familiar with the factors, you'll find it easier to correct and control your spending habits. It will also improve the way you set and enforce your budget.

Your credit card use is an important facet of your credit report. Having such card has its pros and cons. In this book, you'll learn about the different types of credit card, along with their respective pros, cons and requirements. Knowing these things will help you choose the right credit card for your needs and get the best rewards.

If you're not that familiar with credit card application, **this book will provide valuable insight into the tiered system that mainly determines what type you can apply for.** This will save you the time and effort of applying for cards that aren't within your reach. In so doing, you'll avoid the penalties that come with rejected credit card applications.

Aside from getting credit cards, this book will teach you how and how not to use them. As you already know, credit card debt is one of the common causes of financial problems for many adults, not just in the US but in other countries.

This book may not *directly* address how to increase your earnings (it might indirectly do so), but it will definitely help you get the most value out of the money you already have.

Do you want to set up a business? This book will show you how to gain access to startup funding. In case you're not aware, getting a loan isn't the only option – there are so many others!

A list of startup funding sources is included in the last portions of this book. Keep on reading to find out how you should get them and why you should.

Without further ado, let's get right into it!

Congratulations!

The second character of the password required to unlock the Additional Funding Sources Booklet is letter b.

Did You Know?

In 1959, the idea of a "revolving" balance was introduced. This means that cardholders could keep a balance on their credit card without having to pay it off completely every month. While it meant that customers might have to pay finance charges, it also meant that they had more flexibility.

Chapter 1

History and Evolution of Consumer Credit

Consumer credit makes it easier to pay for goods and services when your funds are low. It might seem like a modern invention, but surprisingly, its earliest forms can be traced back to 3500 BC when Sumerians used consumer loans for agricultural purposes.

In 1800 BC, Babylonians had the Code of Hammurabi. The said code contained the first law covering loans. It stated that annual interest rates should only be around 20% for silver and 33.33% for grains. It also required a contract and a public official as a witness.

Around the 8th century, moral concerns over usury became a subject in Europe. The Church even prohibited the practice. But in 1500, explorations and trade missions boosted the demand for loans.

In 1545, England had a law setting the interest rate at 10%. Two centuries later, Jeremy Bentham presented the treatise "A Defense of Usury". His work detailed the possible disadvantages of limiting interest rates. It also challenged the Church's stand against the practice of making money from loans.

England was also the birthplace for credit reporting. In 1803, local tailors traded information about customers who didn't pay their debts. The Manchester Guardian Society was later established in 1826. The said organization published monthly newsletters about people who didn't settle their debts.

New York caught up with the practice of credit reporting when the Mercantile Agency was created in 1841. It devised a system about the assets and characters of local debtors. It was criticized for being subjective and rumor-based.

When the organization got renamed as R. G. Dun and Company, it used an alphanumeric system for determining credit rating. Such practice was implemented until the 1900s.

In 1899, the Retail Credit Company was established in Atlanta. It would later on become Equifax, one of the biggest credit agencies in the US today.

The practice of using modern-day consumer credit became popular when cars became less expensive but were still not that affordable. General Motors Acceptance Corporation (GMAC) was created in 1919. The Detroit-based corporation provided the first installment-based planning for car purchases. This can be deemed as the oldest form of auto loans.

By 1930, more than 60% of car purchases were done by installment. Appliances and furniture sets became cheaper as well. Installment-based payment also became a practice for buying these products.

In 1950s, many middle-class Americans already had plenty of credit information. The creation of BankAmericard (now called Visa) further allowed consumers to buy more even when their funds were low. This led to the accumulation of more information about consumers and their debts.

Years later, computer technologies were used to consolidate data. The Fair Credit Reporting Act was also enacted in the country in 1970s. Equifax, Experian and TransUnion have been the biggest enforcers of such act since 1980s. These credit reporting agencies make use of FICO score and VantageScore in providing information about each consumer.

The Need for a Credit Rating System

These days, it's normal to rely on loans to buy homes, cars, appliances and even groceries. But too much dependence leads to financial troubles for irresponsible consumers. This can also cause problems to the lenders.

That's why the need for a universal credit rating system arose. Credit reporting agencies were established to fill this need.

The main aim of credit reporting agencies is to **understand the risks of accepting loan applications from a certain consumer**. When a consumer has bad credit rating, lenders can take it as a proof to deny loan applications. Some lenders may accept such consumer but they tend to manage the risk by increasing the interest rate.

Somehow, credit reports help consumers become more responsible in paying their debts. After all, a good credit rating makes it easier for them to get loans, apply for credit cards, buy homes and even rent properties.

Types of Consumer Credit

Modern-day consumer credit can be categorized into three: installment, revolving and collections. Also dubbed as consumer debt or consumer loan, this lets consumers borrow money for various goods and services, and repay them for different periods.

Installment

The installment type refers to the way you can manage your debt. Auto loans are the most popular type of this consumer credit. These can also be observed when getting appliances and even Heating, Ventilation and Air Conditioning (HVAC) systems. These loans allow you to buy a vehicle even when you can only give 10% downpayment. After giving the downpayment, you'll be required to pay monthly or quarterly fees to cover the capital and interest rates of your loans.

Mortgages are a lot similar to car loans. But as homes are deemed as assets, loans defaulting on your home or any other real estate property aren't considered as consumer credit. More often than not, products that are purchasable through installment-based consumer credit tend to depreciate after some time. These offerings include groceries, appliances, furniture, clothes, shoes and cars.

There are two ways to get this type of consumer credit. You may apply directly from the establishment or company you're buying from. Another option is to apply for loan from a third-party lending institution or individual.

Revolving

The use of credit card is the most well-known type of revolving consumer credit. It's regarded as revolving because you can keep reusing the card to borrow money and pay for goods and services. With a credit card, consumers can easily purchase different products and services. Unlike the installment type, you'll only need to apply for revolving credit once.

There's a monthly limit on how much credit you can use. This prevents you from excessive use of loans. The limit is mostly dependent on how much you can earn per month. Credit card companies will weigh on your credit rating as well.

Collections

Collections are the final resort when you're unable to pay your debts. Your lenders will seek collection services to ensure that you'll settle your debts whenever you have money. Such services may also get your properties like cars, appliances and furniture especially if you use these as collateral.

The use of consumer credit has its pros and cons. So long as you have self-control, you can be assured that you won't incur too much debt that you can't handle. The rest of this book should equip you with all you need to know in order to make the most out of credit.

Did You Know?

Closing a credit card account in full will have a negative effect on your credit score. Length of history on an account is 15% of your FICO score.

Chapter 2

How to Read, Review and Understand Your Credit Report

If you're applying for a housing loan, trying to get a new credit card or simply curious to know your credit standing, you can send an inquiry and request for a copy of your credit report. But even if you are able to get a hold of one, do you know how to read and understand it?

Your credit report contains a lot of information and it may get difficult to navigate. This chapter will enable you to better understand the report:

What is a credit report, exactly?

A credit report is a compilation of valuable information about you and your finances. It paints a picture of how you handle your credit and debt accounts. It shows how much you owe and how you pay them. It looks at both your current and historical financial status.

In the U.S. there are three credit bureaus or credit reporting agencies that maintain your credit information. They are Equifax, Experian and Trans Union. The companies you do business with send updated debt information to these credit bureaus and they then will update the credit report.

The actual credit report contains several sections that tackle various factors that creditors look at when evaluating your credit viability.

Generally, your credit report will have the following information:

Credit Score

The credit score is a number that represents a consumer's credit worthiness. It shows past and current information about a consumer's credit account.

This is a three-digit number that ranges from 300 to 850 that reflects your creditworthiness to lenders. Creditors use this as a decision-making tool in processing credit applications such as loans and credit cards.

The higher the credit score, the lower the risk for lenders. This metric is discussed in detail in the next chapter.

Personal Identifying information

This section of the credit report includes personally identifying information such as your complete name and known aliases, your social security number, date of birth, contact number and previous and current addresses.

It also includes relevant information on employers as well as employment status.

Credit Account History

This section reflects the history and details of all your credit accounts – both open and closed ones. This is divided into two streams: revolving accounts which includes credit cards, and installment accounts like mortgages or student loads.

Each entry will have the following information: account type, account number, lender, dates opened, credit limit, amount owed and current account status.

Public Record Information

Ideally, this section should be blank. If not, this section will show any open legal issues related to your financial situation. This includes cases of bankruptcy, tax and other liens, judgments and even overdue child support.

These issues have significant negative impact on your credit score.

Inquiries

This section lists the companies that requested your credit report. It would show the inquiry date, the purpose of the inquiry and how long the inquiry will be reflected in your credit report.

Only the following are legally allowed to submit an inquiry:

- Employers,
- Insurance companies,
- Lenders and
- Yourself.

Personal Statement

This section of the report is optional and voluntary. Consumers can make a 100-word statement to dispute presented data, explain your side of the story or alert lenders to an error in dispute. Personal statements do not impact your credit score.

What are the benefits of credit reporting?

Credit reporting is important. No matter where you go, your credit follows you through life. Knowing your credit standing can help you make many decisions about your financial future in many ways.

Your credit report serves as a snapshot of your financial status. It enables you to understand your own financial capacity to commit to credit obligations.

Businesses, lenders, potential employers and landlords can check your credit report to make decisions about you, especially those that relate to financial gains or losses.

With a credit report, you are updated on your level of creditworthiness, which can help you get approvals and better interest rates on loans.

Finally, regularly checking your credit report can help you protect your identity. **You can tell if someone else is using your identity by simply reading the report**. If there are accounts listed that you did not open, you can file a dispute, and then have your credit report reviewed and corrected.

How can you request for copies of your credit report?

All U.S. citizens are entitled to request and receive a free credit report every 12 months from each of the three nationwide credit report companies.

- Equifax (www.equifax.com)
- Experian (www.experian.com)
- Trans Union (www.transunion.com)

These companies created multiple channels in which you can request for a copy. You can go online and check the central website, call a toll-free hotline number or mail a completed form through a P.O. Box. The details of each option is presented below:

- Website: www.annualcreditreport.com

You need to fill out the online order form and submit. The report should be accessible immediately upon requesting

- Toll-Free Number: 1-877-322-8228

After calling the toll-free number, your request will be processed and mailed to you at your noted return address within 15 days

- Mail

You need to submit a completed Annual Credit Report Request Form and mail to: Annual Credit Report Request Service, P.O. Box 105281, Atlanta, GA 30348-5281

Mail requests will be processed and results will be mailed within 15 days of receipt.

Citizens are allowed to order one free copy of your report from each of the reporting companies every 12 months.

Upon requesting, you will need to give your complete legal name, social security number, address and date of birth. Credit reporting companies may request for other information that only you would know, like your loan repayment structure, to validate your identity.

What if there are inaccuracies or incomplete information in your credit report?

If you find errors, inaccuracies or incomplete information in your credit report, you can easily file a dispute with the credit bureau. There are several ways to file a dispute:

- Online dispute through the credit bureau's website:
  - Equifax Disputes: (https://www.equifax.com/personal/disputes/)
  - Experian Disputes: (https://www.experian.com/disputes)
  - Transunion Disputes: (http://www.disputes.transunion.com)

- Send a letter via certified mail to the credit bureau. In your letter, identify what you believe needs to be corrected. Attach a copy of your credit report and highlight the items in question. Include copies of documents that support your claim as well.

As of the moment though, only Trans Union receives dispute via mail. Both Equifax and Experian process all dispute via the online channel.

Send mail to:

TransUnion LLC

Consumer Dispute Center

P.O.Box 2000

Chester, PA 19016

The credit reporting company must investigate the items in question within 30 days upon receipt of dispute. After the investigation is completed and the report is found inaccurate, the company will make the necessary adjustments and notify all credit reporting companies. They must also give you written investigation results and a free copy of the corrected report.

The information in your credit report significantly impacts your life. It is, then, important to ensure that the information declared in that report is accurate and updated. Make it a habit to regularly request for your credit report. Checking every 6- months or once a year should be sufficient. However, if you suspect that someone else is using your identity, then it is best to conduct these checks more frequently.

See the box below for a sample mail you can send to the bureau if you're looking to file for a dispute.

10 November 2018

John H. Smith

1234 Broad Street, New York, NY 10024

Complaint Department

TransUnion LLC

Consumer Dispute Center, P.O.Box 2000

Chester, PA 19016

Dear Sir or Madam:

I recently obtained a copy of my credit report from your agency and found the following item to be in error:

I dispute [VISA credit card] account number [4000 1234 5678 9000]. This account has been paid in full as of September 15, 2018.

I am requesting that the item be updated to correct the information. I've attached copies of the bank statements reflecting the payments I made and supporting my position on this claim. Please investigate this matter and correct the dispute claim as soon as possible.

Sincerely,

John Smith

Enclosures: VISA 4000 1234 5678 9000 September Statement

Did You Know?

Credit cards were originally like today's store cards — offered by individual stores and only for use at those stores. The first one to be used at multiple locations was offered by The Diner's Club in 1950 and it was good for use in 27 restaurants in New York City.

Chapter 3

Understanding Your Credit Score

Your credit score is a powerful number that impacts your present life and your future in a multitude of ways. It is a three-digit number that represents your creditworthiness to lenders. It serves as their guide in approving or disapproving your loan or credit card applications. It also determines the interest rates that will be applied to your mortgages, auto loans and cash loans.

This figure is calculated based on your available credit information. This score is then evaluated by lenders to determine your credibility as a borrower.

A credit score can change from time to time. These changes occur depending on a consumer's financial behavior including when paying a loan. It also takes into account whether the consumer can manage to pay the loan in the long term.

Understanding your credit score helps you determine whether you are keeping your credit healthy. It can also help you keep your credit score in check.

In the US, credit scores are developed using scoring models such as FICO and VantageScore. This section will focus on FICO in particular although VantageScore has its dedicated chapter. This is to provide you a broader view of what's involved in generating credit scores.

The FICO Score

The FICO credit score is the prevailing credit scoring system. It is developed by FICO, a company that specializes in predictive analytics. With this system, they look at a set of credit information to create scores and forecast a consumer's behavior using the same parameters.

FICO Scores gives an accurate prediction of how well a consumer will be able to handle their loans including how they could pay their loans on time and their ability to manage their credit given a higher credit line.

How FICO Scores are Calculated

FICO Scores are calculated based on the following factors. This is just an overview of how the scoring model arrives at your score. These factors will be discussed in detail in Chapter 7.

- Payment history comprises 35% of your score. This reflects how responsible you are with your payments.
- Your total debts make up 30% of the score.
- The duration of your credit history comprises 15%.
- 10% is allocated to current or new credit inquiries.
- The last 10% goes to the diversity of your credit accounts.

Other score models also use the same factors. Therefore, a good FICO score indicates that that you are likely to also get a good score on other credit score standards.

What's a Good FICO Score?

Anything that's at least 670 is considered a good FICO rating. Nonetheless, you should still aim for a higher score because it can give you better interests when applying for loans and discounts when buying real estate, among other benefits as will be discussed in a short while.

The FICO Score Range

Your FICO score can fall between 300 and 850 with the lower number representing more risk for the lender. A good credit score makes it possible to buy your dream home, your own luxury vehicle or open a business. A bad score, usually less than 500, may present challenges in attaining the same things.

Poor (300-559)

Scores that fall within this range are way under the standard score. If you're in this range, it shows lenders that giving you a loan is risky. You probably won't be able to get loan applications approved except perhaps when there's collateral.

Fair (580 – 669)

This is the gray zone. It's still under the standard score of consumers but you still won't get great credit deals. If you're in this range, some lenders may approve loan requests. In fact, some of them will still consider this a poor score. However, you may still get subprime loans especially if there are extenuating circumstances

Good (670 - 739)

Many consumers have a credit score that falls within this range. Most lenders will see this as an acceptable score because it's not risky. Only about 8% of applicants with a score that fall within this range are likely to become seriously delinquent.

Very Good (740-799)

This score is higher than the standard score of consumers. If your score is in this range, lenders can see that you are a responsible consumer and you'll be getting good interest rates.

Excellent 800-850

This score is way higher than the standard score of consumers. In this range the lenders see that you are an excellent consumer.

The FICO Score Range was recently updated to FICO Score 9, but most lenders still use the old FICO score range.

The Importance of a Good Credit Score

There are many ways in which a good credit score can benefit you as a consumer.

1. Higher chances of loan approval

A good credit score increases your chances of getting your loan applications approved, and the process will be faster too. A good credit score tells lenders that you are diligent in paying your dues. This indicates that you are not a risky 'investment' and this attracts lenders to do business with you.

2. Getting the best credit card deals

Banks will likely approve your credit card application because a good score reassures banks that you can handle your credit and pay your bills on time.

3. Lower interest rates.

Interest costs money so having good credit that helps you get the lowest interest rate possible saves a lot of money in the long run. And since lenders will see you as a reliable investment, you are likely to get the best structured loans.

4. Higher credit limits

The increase in credit limit due to good credit scores will not only allow you more access to credit. It will also improve your credit utilization ratio, which means even better credit scores. Just be careful about requesting for a higher credit limits though because it usually means that the issuer will perform a hard inquiry, which will factor into your credit score.

5. More bargaining power

A good credit score allow you to negotiate for the best loan structures. This is because banks and lenders see you as a guaranteed business and asset that can return in the future.

6. Better car insurance premiums

Many states ban the practice of car insurance providers using credit scores to assess insurance premiums. However, in states where it is allowed, most insurers will check your score and reward those with higher scores because they believe that those who have good credit are predisposed to behavior that reduces risk.

7. Better Rates for Mortgage Loans

When you're buying something as high-priced as real estate, a small difference in interest rates, say between% 4 and 4.25%, can add up.

8. Getting Rental Approvals

Renting an apartment will be easier with a good credit score. Landlords look at your credit score to see if you can assure on-time payments on rent.

9. Less Security Deposits

You will be asked to pay less deposit or none at all when acquiring a new apartment or phone. This is because a good credit score indicates that you are a low-risk tenant/customer and will be likely to pay your bills on time.

10. Better quality of life

This is the best reason why you want a good credit score. You don't have to worry about your landlord coming to evict you from your home. You would want to get your loan applications approved if you need to build that dream house. A life with less stress can make you happier than most.

Downside of having a low credit score

A good credit score will help you in the long term because you can get prime deals with lenders and banks. A low credit score on the hand can become a nightmare and will cause you so much stress and difficulties in the long run.

1. Having your loans declined

Lenders and banks will likely decline loans made with a low credit score. This is due to the risky nature of lending your money.

2. High Interest Rates

Low credit scores show the probability of a consumer of being delinquent. A lender or bank might let such an individual to borrow from them with the caveat that the interest rates are higher and the credit line is smaller. After all, they will be cautious in lending your money.

3. Declined credit card applications and low credit limit

Credit card companies usually look for consumers who can use their cards well. Delinquent payments and going over the credit limit are a no-no. These practices can lead to low credit scores, which in turn, increase the probability of having your credit card application declined.

Even if you get a credit card application approved, it will still have a low credit limit. Banks will be wary of giving you a higher credit limit for fear of you not paying your dues.

4. High deposits and difficulty in renting apartments

Landlords may check an individual's credit score to determine if he should charge a deposit. This is especially true for well-established landlords in prime lots and areas. If you have a poor credit score which indicates that you are more likely to be unable to pay rent, he may require an even bigger security deposit to compensate for the risk. You may have to end up renting a place in in less desirable areas.

5. Setting up a small business will be a challenge

You'll probably need a loan from the bank in putting up a business. Banks are likely to be reluctant to lend start-up money to those with low credit score. What they like to see is your ability to pay on time.

6. Finding a job can be a challenge

Some companies take your credit score into consideration when running a background check because of the nature of the job. Potential employees who are going to work for financial institutions are also asked about their credit scores. This is because some employees believe that credit scores indicate whether or not someone is able to handle responsibilities.

7. Higher Insurance Premiums

Low credit score can play a part in getting home or car insurance with higher premium. Insurance companies experience more claims from clients with lower credit scores than most. They fear people who have low credit score to file fraudulent claims.

8. Difficulty in getting a new car

Getting a new car with a low credit score will also be difficult. Car companies can decline your car loan when they see that your credit history indicates poor credit. This is indicated by delinquent payments on your car loan and repossession.

9. Difficulty buying a house.

Banks and lenders check a consumer's ability to pay for their home loans. Foreclosures, repossessions, and delayed payments in your history will decrease your chances of getting a home loan.

10. Calls from debt collectors

A life spent hounded by the constant ringing of the phone is not ideal. But it may become norm if you have bad credit, as banks and lenders will ask collectors to go after you.

What to do if you have no FICO Score

At the start, you may not have credit yet. But building your credit score may not be as hard as you think.

The first option is to become an authorized user on someone else's credit card. This is likely going to be your parents. You can set up an agreement with your parent on how you can pay for your purchases. Remember that you won't be legally obligated to pay for them but if the primary shareholder expects you to pay your share, then do so. Ask the card issuer if they report authorized user activity.

You can also ask other people to co-sign a loan or credit card line. This will in turn help you understand the responsibilities of having credit. Co-signing with them requires you to pay half of the dues.

You may also apply for loan for credit-building. This loan has the sole purpose of building credit, which makes it perfect for those who have little to no history. It works like a savings account in which you will not really "borrow" money in the strictest sense of the word. You will be periodically paying an amount and your payments will be reported to the credit bureaus. You can then collect the money after the "loan" is repaid. You can start your search online. Credit unions and community banks are the ones that usually offer these. It might take a while to find one because they're not widely advertised.

Fourth, you can build credit through secured credit cards. Secured credit cards require you to have an initial deposit equal to your credit limit. They are used for a limited time.

Finally, you can build credit through rent. Ask your landlord if he reports your rent to authorized rent trackers. Some scoring models do not include this in their calculation, but then some lenders do consider them.

How to achieve a 700+ credit score

It is possible to achieve a 700+ credit score if you do the following:

1. Build good credit right at the start.

Pay your dues on time and pay them in full. It will definitely help in increasing your credit score. Take into account that the FICO Score puts heavy weight on this.

2. Use your credit well.

Do not go over your credit limit. It is wise to use as little of your credit as possible. This will show that you have good control in money expenditure.

3. Avoid getting hard inquiries.

Note that hard inquiries lower your score. Soft inquiries are fine. To manage this, only apply for a new credit account if you absolutely need it.

4. Use various credit accounts.

It is a good idea to have various credit accounts provided you are able to handle them well. Additionally, mixed accounts can also be a benefit. It will show how well you are able to manage different types of accounts and still be able to pay for them all.

5. Avoid closing accounts too soon.

Having various accounts can be beneficial if you manage them well. It is better to close them if you don't. But be careful because the duration of the account also factor into your score. Also, make sure you don't close several accounts all at the same time. This may hurt your credit score. Don't remove your oldest account because it will contribute to your credit history.

6. Avoid having negative marks.

Negative credit information can lower your credit scores. Foreclosures, repossessions and a history of delayed payments are negative marks. Review and check your credit score from time to time. Make sure to report any error in your credit history to avoid the lowering of your credit score.

As we go through the next few chapters, you will learn more about how your financial behavior can affect your credit scores and what you can do to maintain healthy credit. For now, remember that consistency is the key. Be diligent and handle your credits well. In time your credit score will increase and reach a score of 700.

Did Your Know?

Mastercard began life as MasterCharge and was formed by four Californian banks in 1967. It became Mastercard in 1979 and it was the first card to use holograms.

Chapter 4

Monitoring Credit Reports and Credit Scores

Credit monitoring safeguards consumers from possible fraud. They secure accounts from identity theft issues and suspicious activities.

What are credit-monitoring services?

Credit monitoring services allow consumers to track their credit report and credit score. Through this type of service, consumers are notified of any changes in their accounts. The notice comes in the form of e-mails or text alerts.

Among the activities that automatically alert consumers are as follows:

- New account openings (e.g., credit cards and loans)
- New credit inquiries
- New public records (i.e., information on bankruptcies, court judgments)
- Changes in home address
- Late payments and/or unpaid debts

How to check your credit score

There are many ways to find out a credit score. It can be checked by the consumer manually. It can also be determined with the help of agencies or through various online resources.

For the manual procedure, a consumer may look through his financial statements. These may be from credit cards, financial institutions, or loan statements. Consumers can also opt to log in to their online accounts to check their credit score.

Consumers can also use credit score services from sites. This, however, may come at a price. Some credit scoring sites offer credit scores for free. While others require their customers to pay monthly subscription fee.

Consumers are not limited to these options. They can also check their credit score from agencies or from specific online sites. Among the agencies that provide this kind of service are Equifax, Experian, and TransUnion. These agencies use credit scoring models to determine a consumer's credit score. They also make use of various data to calculate credit scores.

If you're from the US, you can also go to www.annualcreditreport.com to check your credit scores. The site provides a copy of credit report from major credit bureaus. Consumers can get a copy of their credit scores at least once in every 12 months. Revisit the previous chapter to get more information on how to get your credit score

Hard and Soft Credit Inquiries

Hard Inquiry occurs when a prospective lender looks into a consumer's credit report. This type of inquiry helps a lender determine whether the consumer qualifies for a loan. It happens when a consumer applies for a credit card, car loan, or mortgage.

On the other hand, a Soft Inquiry is when a person or company does a background check on a consumer's credit report. Soft Inquiry is done so that a lender can determine whether the consumer is still creditworthy. The lender checks for signs of risk on lending matters. Soft Inquiry can be done without the consumer's permission.

These types of credit inquiries both check one's credit score. They only differ on the impact they have on the credit score itself.

While Soft Inquiry does not have any effect on a credit, Hard Inquiry does. Hard Inquiry slightly lowers credit scores. It also remains on a consumer's account record for two years. This is what consumers should be concerned about.

Numerous hard inquiries could indicate two things. One, a consumer may be desperate for credit. Or two, he did not succeed in borrowing from previous creditors for whatever reason.

Because of these, it would be best for consumers to maintain low records of hard inquiries. Large volumes of hard inquiries mean high level of risk. As a result, lenders become wary of potential clients with numerous records. Worse, lenders might reject them since they are perceived to be more likely to file for bankruptcy in the future.

Types of monitoring services available

It is important to maintain a healthy credit report and score since they determine a consumer's creditworthiness. Credit monitoring services help consumers check their credit reports and scores.

There are numerous credit monitoring firms offering services to consumers. The three major credit bureaus (Equifax, Experian, and TransUnion) also provide monitoring services. Other monitoring services can be accessed online through www.annualcreditreport.com.

Some of the best monitoring services available are Identity Guard, Credit Karma, and Identity Force.

Identity Guard provides protection against identity theft. It has a mobile app that notifies consumers of changes in their credit records. It allows consumers to check their credit reports monthly from the three major credit bureaus. Identity Guard also comes with a million dollars' worth of insurance against identity theft.

Credit Karma, on the other hand, offers free monitoring services. It allows consumers access to credit reports at any time. Compared to Identity Guard, Credit Karma provides consumers access to only two of the major credit bureaus – TransUnion and Equifax. Here, credit report is updated weekly.

Identity Force is the monitoring service with the most security features. In addition to identity monitoring and credit monitoring services, Identity Force also monitors consumer's personal information. It also notifies consumers whether their accounts have been compromised. It also comes with an insurance policy worth $1 million.

Credit information services such as monitoring, credit scoring, or applications that oversee accounts, may come at a hefty price. However, they're crucial in this day and age where there is so much data mining that occur all over the world.

Did You Know?

It is against the merchant agreements of Mastercard, Visa, and American Express for a vendor to require you to provide your phone number, home address or other personal information. You also do not need to present a driver's license or spend above a certain purchase amount.

Congratulations!

The fourth character of the password required to unlock the Additional Funding Sources Booklet is letter z.

Chapter 5

The VantageScore Model

Equifax, Experian and TransUnion collaborated to develop and introduce a new credit score model that can compete with the FICO model - the VantageScore. The process for FICO and VantageScore are almost the same but with a slight difference on the outcome of the credit scores.

What is a good VantageScore?

In VantageScore 3.0's scoring model, scores range from 300-850. A rating of 700 and above is considered good, while a rating of 750 and above is considered excellent.

However, VantageScore 4.0 is going to be released very soon.

VantageScore Ranges Explained

A credit score of 300-549 is rated as very poor and applicants with this number are unlikely to be extended credit.

550-649 credit score is rated as poor and applicants in this range could be extended some credit but they may experience certain conditions such as larger down payments.

A credit rating between 650 and 699 is rated as Fair that allows an applicant for credit but they are unlikely to get a competitive rate.

A score of 700-749 is good. Credit applications from people with this rating are accepted and come at competitive rates.

Lastly, a credit score of 750-850 is rated as excellent and applicants with these scores get the best and most competitive rates on credit accounts.

How VantageScore calculates your credit score

VantageScore categorizes credit information into six. These categories have different levels of influence on your credit scores. Here is how VantageScore groups the importance of credit score data:

- Payment history: extreme influence
- Age and type of credit: high influence
- Percentage of used credit limit: high influence
- Total balances and debt: moderate influence
- Recent credit behavior and inquiries: less influence
- Available credit: less influence

Differences between the FICO and VantageScore Models

FICO and VantageScore are the most known credit-scoring models offered by different Credit Reporting Agencies. The process for FICO and VantageScore are almost the same but there are some differences in rules and processes.

1. Length of Credit History required

In order to get a FICO score, the consumer must already have an existing one or more credit accounts that have already been reported to the rightful credit-scoring agency. It must have been open for the last six months and been reported within the last six months.

VantageScore, on the other hand, allows applications from consumers with one month of credit history so long as it is an account reported within the last two years.

Because of this, VantageScore can provide information to consumers who did not qualify with FICO, thereby offering convenience.

2. Significance of Late Payments

Your late payments matter both to your FICO and VantageScore accounts. They both look into these records:

- When did your last late payment occur?
- In how many of your accounts did late payments occur?
- How many payments on an account have you missed?

Late payments have an impact on your credit score, but the difference between these models is that, FICO penalizes these late payments equally. While in VantageScore, late payments for mortgages give a huge disadvantage to   consumers. So if you've been having problems with your mortgage, you might have a better FICO score than in VantageScore.

3. Impact of Credit Inquiries

Deduplications happen when a consumer inquires for credit loans in which lenders send the application to other lenders, causing your account to reflect multiple inquiries. The difference is that FICO uses a 45-day span to deduplicate your inquiries while VantageScore only gives a 14-day span. Be wary of credit inquiry especially when you are planning for a house or car loan because it might become a "hard inquiry" that can lower your credit score.

4. Effect of Low-Balance Collections

When your account is given to a collection agency, FICO ignores all the collections that have a balance lower than $100. As for VantageScore, it ignores the collections regardless of the original balance of the account.

Did You Know?

A fixed interest rate on a credit card can be changed with only 15 days notice from the credit card provider.

Chapter 6

Factors That Impact Your Credit Rating

Improving your credit score requires understanding the factors that impact your score. Having this information will help you make informed financial decisions that will impact your score. Remember, the higher your credit score, the better the chance of getting the credit you need.

Note that FICO and VantageScore have fundamentally different methodologies in coming up with your credit score. FICO, however, is the more ubiquitous which is why their system was used as basis for this chapter.

Nonetheless, here's a chart that should give a quick overview of the similarities and differences of the two

Fico Score Weights	Vantage Score Weights
Payment History 35%	Payment History 40%
Credit Utilization 30%	Credit Utilization 20%
Age of Credit Accounts 15%	Age and Diversity of Credit accounts 21%
Credit Diversity 10%	Total Balances/Debt 11%
New Credit 10%	New Credit and Available Credit 8%

But essentially, there are five key factors that impact your credit score. They are payment history, credit utilization, the age of accounts, credit diversity and recent credit history. Together these factors define the characteristics of the borrower. It estimates the chance of default and assess the risk of a potential financial loss to the lender.

Payment History

Credit Score Weight: 35%

Payment history is the most important factor in calculating your credit score. This usually makes up a good part of your score. It is a measure of your ability to settle your bills on schedule.

Your past long-term paying trend is used to forecast future long-term behavior. Generally, missing your due date for a couple of days isn't so bad. Still, you should make it a habit to pay bills on time. Note that you may be charged late payment fees or reconnection fees to have services back. And that's not the only bad thing that comes with late payment.

Your credit score will be affected when companies report a late payment incident to the credit bureau. FICO, for example, will note this incident and consider other factors to determine how your action will impact your score.

They will be looking at your most recent reported missed due date incident, review the frequency of late payments in the past and aggregate the amount owed from all your credit accounts.

Serious payment related issues such as irregular payments, collections, repossessions, or a foreclosure can destroy your credit score and make it extremely difficult to get approved for anything that would require good credit.

To improve your credit score:

Make sure that you make all your bill payments on time each month. To do this, you can set-up payment reminders in your calendar, revise payment due date to align with your paycheck or enroll your accounts to an auto-pay service. These actions will automate the manual task of remembering to settle your bills on time.

If you have a tendency to forget or struggle to make payments on time, consider setting your accounts for automatic payments.

You can request to change your bill due dates to better align with your paycheck.

Credit Utilization

Credit Score Weight: 30%

Credit utilization is the ratio of your balance to the total credit available. To simplify, it is the amount of the credit that you are actually using.

Note that FICO looks at credit utilization in two parts. First, you'll get a separate credit utilization score for each of your credit cards. Then, your total credit utilization will be calculated in which your total balance is compared to your total credit limit. If you get a bad score in any of the two categories, your credit score could be damaged. This means that you should keep an eye not just on one account but all of them. Even if you handled a few of them really well but overlooked one or two, you could be in for a poor score.

To get a good credit utilization score, you should maintain low credit card balances. Those who habitually max out credit cards or almost always reach their credit limit tend to be viewed as a potentially irresponsible debtor and therefore a risk.

With credit utilization, the guideline is "the lower, the better." Having high balances will heavily impact your credit score. So to keep within acceptable limits, try not to go over 30% of your available credit. To illustrate, if you have $1,000 credit card limit, you should use no more than $300 monthly. Apply this 30% guideline to the total combined limit of all your available credit.

To improve this aspect of your credit score:

The simplest way is to manage your spending habits. Be careful when requesting a credit limit increase in your existing accounts because it's a hard inquiry and can therefore lower your credit score. Make early payments throughout your billing cycle if you are not able to do the first two options.

Age of Accounts

Credit Score Weight: 15%

This refers to the average age of your credit accounts. To measure this, lenders take into account three things: the average age of all accounts from open date to the present, the age of the earliest opened account and the age of the most recently opened account. To compute the average age of your accounts, scoring models sum up the months of all the accounts in your credit report (this is from the open date to the present) and then divide the total by the number of accounts.

A long-established credit history provides a clearer snapshot of your long-term financial behavior. So, as a principle: "the lengthier your credit history, the better the score." But those that don't have long histories can still garner great credit scores if they have consistent on-time payments and have low utilization ratios.

To improve your credit score:

Raise the average age of your accounts by avoiding the practice of constantly opening new accounts. Only do it if you absolutely have to. But if you already have new ones, let them age; don't close them just yet.

Leave your oldest accounts open and active. This will show your ability to manage credit over time.

Think carefully before canceling your cards or closing credit accounts especially those that you've had for some time. Long standing accounts can positively influence your credit score.

Credit Mix

Credit Score Weight: 10%

Creditors prefer consumers that maintain a diverse credit mix. People who hold different types of credit accounts can get a high credit score. Having varied accounts show that you are able to effectively manage multiple types of loans.

Credit accounts include installment loans and revolving credit. Installment loans such as student loans, auto loans, home equity loans, signature loans, credit builder loans and mortgages usually involve a fixed monthly payment and a scheduled repayment structure.

Revolving credit accounts include credit cards and home equity lines of credit. With this type of credit, there's usually a set limit that you can borrow from regularly. People with no credit cards tend to be viewed as higher risk compared to those that are able to manage their cards responsibly.

To improve your credit score:

Consider getting installment loans. A personal installment loan may be helpful. You may also opt for a low-rate auto loan and then just pay it off as soon as possible. Even if you pay it in just a few months, it would still count as an installment loan.

Try not to do business with finance companies. Their rates and terms are not as good as those from banks and credit unions.

Get a credit card. Keep a low or even no balance. If you have poor or no credit score, you can still get a secured credit card.

Apply for and open new credit accounts only as needed.

Recent Credit History

Credit Score Weight: 10%

New or recent credit is important because it can make you seem like a risky investment to lenders.

Here are the factors that are considered under this category.

- The accounts you've opened in the last 6 to 12 months
- The ratio of new accounts to old ones
- The number of credit inquiries particularly hard inquiries and how long it's been since the last one
- How long it has been since you opened the newest account
- The reappearance of positive credit information for an account that used to reflect payment problems

To improve your credit score:

Open a new account or two but do not overdo it. Remember that if you open too many accounts, the hard inquiries will show up on your report and damage your score. Only consider what you need and apply for a loan when the time is right. Be patient and build your credit score over time.

It is good to note that inquiries completely disappear from your credit report after 24 months. Only inquiries made in the last 12 months factor into your credit score. So, try to review your credit rating periodically and keep yourself updated.

Avoid regularly opening new credit accounts.

Open new credit accounts with long intervals between each application. Avoid opening multiple accounts over a short period of time.

The Bottomline

These factors are considered in all credit score models. Knowing the weights placed on each factor will give you a better idea on where to focus your attention.

In this case, with a total of 65% weight in computing for your credit score, credit history and credit utilization are the needle movers. This basically means that you need to do these three things right now to help manage your credit score. These are things that you have direct control over and can easily handle.

Lastly, remember that it is important to check your own credit report regularly. It is a smart move especially if you aim to keep a healthy credit score. These personal and soft inquiries don't cost a thing and don't affect your credit rating. It also gives you a better view of your financial standing real-time.

Did You Know?

A common clause in the terms and conditions is that the cardholder waives their right to sue the credit card company.

Chapter 7

Factors That Do Not Affect Your Credit Score

Those who are worrying that their credit scores are affected by every financial decision they make may be in for a surprise. Here are some factors that do not affect your credit scores.

Income

Your credit reports do record your employment history but it doesn't affect your credit scores, neither does your current income. Keep in mind, though, that your income may have an effect on how you are paying your bills, because this one does impact your credit scores.

If you have applied for a loan before, you'll remember that you were asked to provide information regarding the amount of your monthly income through your employment certificate and copies of your pay slips and income tax returns. These only influence the maximum amount of loan you can get but not your credit scores.

Age

Age does not impact your credit scores although the credit reports do record your day of birth. However, 15% of your total credit score is related to the age of the accounts you have at the moment.

Marital Status

Credit reports record your marriage status as well as the name of your spouse but neither affect credit scores. Your credit scores also don't merge or link with your spouse's when you tie the knot. Each of you will have separate credit scores and reports.

Education

Whether you graduate from Harvard or from some online education system, it won't be recorded in the credit reports. Neither will the degree program you completed. But some lenders may consider your educational attainment and the employment which you acquired through your background. This might be part of their application process.

Location

Your credit reports have your place of residence but it won't be used in scoring your credit. Your location might have impact on your insurance rates as well as property taxes but not on your credit standing.

Criminal Record

If you go to jail, your credit reports will have a notation of the event but your credit scores remain the same. However, some other factors arising from you being getting some jail time might significantly affect your credit standing. These include civil judgments like overdue child support, tax liens, monetary judgments due to collection accounts, and bankruptcy. Also, court costs and fines that you are not able to settle on time and sent to collections will appear on the reports.

Net Worth

Just like your income, the amount of assets under your name can help you get a bigger loan amount but if you already have a bad credit score, you won't get approved. However, liens you have on your house like mortgage will appear on credit reports.

Debit Cards

Debit card activities don't get reported to credit agencies so you won't get to build credit if you keep using debit cards on your favorite restaurants and stores. The same applies to cash and checks. Your credit card is the only plastic that impacts your credit score.

Gender and Religion

These are some types of information that you need to put in when applying for loans and credit cards and they are recorded in your credit reports but whether you're a male or female, Christian or Muslim, does not impact your credit scores.

Did You Know?

There is an online dating service called CreditScoreDating.com for those who are concerned with the financial situation of a potential mate. The site's motto is "Credit Scores Are Sexy".

Chapter 8

Credit Cards

So What Exactly Is A Credit Card? A credit card is a type of payment card. It is issued to allow users or cardholders to pay for goods and services without the use of cash. The amount that you can spend is based on the credit card agreement that you have signed. In the future, you are obliged to pay the agreed amount and the charges that come with it.

How Credit Cards Work (Consumer Side)

The card issuer, which is usually a bank, grants a line of credit to you and creates a revolving account. MasterCard and Visa are some of the most popular payment processors for credit cards. The issuing bank provides the necessary paperwork for the user or soon-to-be card holder before he or she can acquire a payment card.

The revolving account represents the debts of the borrower. The outstanding balance or the unpaid, interest-bearing balance of a loan portfolio doesn't have to be paid fully every month.

However, every month, the credit card holder may be required to pay a specific minimum amount based on the amount of money owed to the lender or bank. Nevertheless, the user can pay the issuer any amount between the full balance and the minimum payment.

If he or she can't deposit the minimum payment required at the end of the monthly billing period, the remaining monthly balance will roll over into the following month.

In this case, the issuer will charge the holder with an interest that is based on the required monthly minimum payment. The interest will be added to the remaining balance.

How Credit Cards Work (Business Side)

A card issuer, such as a credit union or a bank, enters into a deal or an agreement with merchants so that they will accept their payment cards. Merchants advertise the type of cards they accept. They display acceptance marks.

With respect to credit cards, an acceptance mark is a design or logo that indicates the card schemes that a merchant or ATM accepts. In restaurants, this is particularly indicated at the bottom of the menu.

The issuer provides the card to the customer after or during the time that the credit provider approves the account of the borrower. The provider need not be the same business entity as the issuer.

After receiving the card, the user can utilize it to pay for certain goods and services. The user consents to pay by entering his or her PIN or by signing a receipt. The receipt contains the details of the card and indicates the amount that has to be paid.

Nowadays, many merchants accept verbal authorizations (i.e. electronic) by means of the internet or through a telephone. Electronic authorization is also known as CNP or Card Not Present Transaction.

A CNP, Mail Order or Telephone Order is a transaction made in which the cardholder can't present the card for a seller's visual examination. Electronic verification systems enable merchants to validate whether the presented card is valid or not and to verify whether or not the cardholder has enough credits for the requested service or item.

The verification or transaction is performed using a point-of-sale, or a credit card payment terminal. The card's data, such as the name of the user and the available credits, is obtained from a chip or a magnetic stripe on the card.

For CNP transactions, in which the card can't be physically presented or confirmed, merchants will also validate that the client owns the card. They do this by asking for the security code, the customer's billing address, and the card's date of expiry. The security code is printed at the back of the card.

Credit Card Versus Line of Credit

A revolving account represents the actual debt and its generated interest every payment period, whereas, a line of credit or LOC is a credit source that is extended to a business, individual, or government by a financial institution. There are many forms of line of credit. It can come in the form of overdraft line of credit, traditional revolving credit card account, and term loans.

In other words, an LOC can be a source of funds. It is an arrangement between a customer and a financial institution. It establishes the maximum amount that the client can borrow. He or she can access funds from the LOC anytime.

However, the borrower can't spend or withdraw more than the maximum amount set. This can also happen when the borrower fails to meet requirements like timely payments.

Cash Advances

Generally, a credit card allows the holder to borrow money as a cash advance or as payment to a merchant or entity. A cash advance is a short-term loan from a financial institution such as a bank or any alternative lender. Most credit card issuers provide this service.

With a cash advance, the cardholder can withdraw cash either over the counter or through ATM. Cash advances incur a fee of more or less 5% of the debt. Often, the interest is higher than other forms of credit card transactions.

Depending on the guidelines included in the agreement, there are specific purchases made using a credit card which are considered to be cash advances. Examples are prepaid debit cards, lottery tickets, gaming chips, and certain fees and taxes paid to the government. Such transactions also have a high-interest rate and don't have a grace period.

There are times when merchants fail to disclose the actual nature of a transaction. In this case, the deal is processed as a standard credit card transaction.

Often, merchants pass the processing fees on to the cardholders despite the guidelines. In some agreements, it is indicated that users must not incur extra fees for paying using a credit card.

Billing and Payment

Every month, the user receives a statement that indicates the total amount owed, any outstanding fees, and the transactions made using the card. The cardholder must pay a specified minimum amount every month in order to avoid incurring additional charges.

If the holder fails to pay the defined minimum portion of the debt, the issuer will impose penalties such as late fees.

To mitigate this, financial institutions often organize for automatic payments. Through automatic payments, the monthly payment is deducted from the user's bank account. As long as the user has enough funds, automatic payments help the cardholder mitigate penalties and additional fees.

Also, as of today, many banks offer electronic statements so you can access your bill anytime as soon as it's released. This serves as an addition if not a replacement to physical statements.

Electronic statements can be checked by logging in to the user's account on the issuer's online banking site. The notification for every new statement is sent to the user's email address.

If the issuer allows it, the user can have other options such as electronic fund transfer for paying the debt apart from a physical check. Depending on the card issuer, the user can also make multiple payments during one billing cycle.

Credit Card Pros and Cons

Pros

Why should you get one? Here are some reasons.

1. More purchasing options

The use of cash is often only limited to in-person purchases unless, of course, you choose the Cash on Delivery option when ordering a product online. With a credit card, you can order via the internet or the phone.

2. Convenience

Credit cards are more convenient to use compared to cash and checks. You don't have to bring a ton of cash with you when shopping and by just swiping your card, you are done with a transaction. In metropolitan areas, cities, and suburban towns, many establishments accept credit cards. This implies that you need not stop by an ATM to pay for what you need. However, there are places that don't allow customers to give tip via a credit card.

3. Pay in Installments

While it's advised to pay your debt fully each month, you can pay your balance in installments over a specified period of time. It's useful when you find yourself short of money.

4. Build credit

If you use your credit card correctly, which means paying on time, maintaining the minimum balance, and keeping your balance low, among others you can build a good credit score. (More on this in the next section). A good credit score is useful when you need to apply for an auto loan or when you need financing to buy a house or start a business.

5. Emergency funds

Using credit cards to cover emergency expenses is not recommended. However, there are times that a credit card can cover small unexpected expenses, which is especially handy if you don't have enough savings.

6. Earn rewards

If you pay on time and you don't incur penalties, you will earn rewards that you can utilize for gift cards, credit card miles, or cash. You can earn rewards by using your credit card often and by paying on time. Nonetheless, this should never be the sole reason for getting a card.

7. All the perks of using plastic without paying interest charges

Some credit cards have 0% interest on balance transfers and purchases for the first six months. This enables you to pay your debt over time without incurring additional charges. In addition, if you settle your total balance each month, you can enjoy the convenience and flexibility that credit cards offer without worrying about interest fees.

8. No loss of access to funds

If someone accesses your checking account without authorization, they can drain all the balance in it. In this case, you must wait for a certain period of time for the processing of your fraudulent report before you receive your lost funds. With a credit card, you must wait for the processing period also. But at least, you can access your account and still make purchases using your credit card.

9. You have the right to withhold payment

There are times when credit card users experience some type of billing error. This can include unauthorized charges. Unauthorized charges may include a charge that is listed on your monthly account statement with the wrong amount or date, a charge for an item that was not delivered. You may receive a billing error when the issuer fails to update a payment made by you. When you experience this, you have the right to file a report. You can dispute it with the issuer. Meanwhile, you need not pay for the error.

Cons

Using a credit card has many benefits, but there are some downsides, namely:

1. Uncontrolled spending

A credit card gives people the illusion that they have more money than what they really have. It encourages many people to spend more than they can afford.

It gives you additional purchasing power, so you might be tempted to buy things that are out of your league.

Studies showed that credit card holders are more willing to go over their balance than other people.

2. Reduce future income

Each time you apply for a loan or each time you use your credit card, you are borrowing money with interest. You haven't earned that money yet, and you are obliged to pay it in the future. A small portion or a large chunk of your income may go towards the payment for your credit card balance.

3. It can be confusing

For people who are totally new to credit card agreements, the terms and conditions can be confusing. If you plan to become a credit card holder, you must understand the technical terms so that you can use it correctly and be free from penalties.

4. Interest and fees are expensive

Depending on the type of credit card you have and on the way you utilize it, you may incur hundreds of dollars' worth of interest and fees during the course of one year. This is the reason why you have to understand credit card terms and to know how to avoid penalties and fees.

5. Credit card fraud

Owning a credit card makes you vulnerable to credit card fraud. Thieves and hackers don't need to steal your card to acquire your information and use your balance. By hacking the online shop where you have used your card, they can steal your personal information. They can use it to purchase goods or services. They get the item while you receive the debt.

6. You pay without cash but you generate debt

Each time you avail or purchase something using a credit card, you generate debt. And each time you miss a due date, your debt increases.

7. Misuse ruins your credit score

Your credit score is directly tied to how you utilize your credit card. If you fail to meet agreements, your credit score is affected.

8. How are they useful when trying to build a credit score?

Lenders perform a valuation of their clients so that they can determine whether or not a client can avail a particular loan such as an auto or mortgage loan or be able to repay his or her debts. They need to know your creditworthiness.

Your credit score evaluates your creditworthiness. It is based on your credit history, which in turn reflects your ability to pay.

Now, at the beginning, you probably won't have any credit score from FICO. After all, you won't have any record with the credit Bureau if you have not engaged in any traceable transaction that can serve as proof that you can pay loans.

By getting a credit card, you can get started. Credit card companies will report your payment activity to the credit bureau. Remember that payment history makes up 35% of FICO scores and you can start getting that good payment history going by using your credit card and paying your monthly credit card dues.

If you already have a credit score albeit a poor one and you want to show the credit bureaus that you've steered your finances back on track, you can start by using your credit card and then paying your bills diligently. In just a few years, you will be able to start building that credit.

To build credit with your credit card, remember to:

- Pay in full and on time

- Treat your credit card as a debit card

- Remember to keep your balance low

- Keep your accounts open

All these tips are in keeping with the principles that help you keep healthy credit.

Types of Credit Cards

The first credit cards made during the 1950s had 1 feature only – they allow you to carry out business with an establishment and then get a monthly bill, much like utilities. They were also initially offered only to the wealthy.

Nowadays, credit cards are distinct from each other in many ways. Each type may differ from another when it comes to fees, rewards programs, and interest rates.

Before choosing your credit card, it's crucial to know the best one for your lifestyle and financial situation.

1. Vanilla credit cards

Vanilla credit cards are also known as standard credit cards. It has no special features, perks, or annual fee. Its credit limit depends on the user's creditworthiness. This is ideal for students, new credit card users and low-income individuals.

Pros

- Cheaper than other cards

- Simple and easy to use

- Easy to apply

- Low interest rate

Cons
- Not flexible
- Usually no additional offers or features

2. Reward Cards

Reward cards are credit cards that offer incentives to purchase certain products or services. You get points for every dollar spent and you can exchange them for rewards, hence the name. They are usually made accessible through a store or group of stores that allows clients to get price reductions according to the amount that they spend.

These cards are ideal for frequent travellers and those who like shopping. There are many kinds of rewards cards and the 5 most common are:

- Cash back cards,

- General reward points cards,

- Retail rewards cards,

- Gas cards, and

- Travel credit cards.

Cardholders don't have to settle for just one rewards credit card. Having more than one card in your wallet gives you the opportunity to earn more rewards. It is wise to have one credit card that pays high rewards on gas purchases and another one for travel purchases.

Pros
- Earn points while spending

- Travel for free

- Enjoy exclusive perks

Cons
- High interest rates
- High annual fees

How to travel for free using your credit card

You can charge the travel expenses on the card and redeem the travel points as statement credits. You can also use cashback (i.e. earn back a certain percentage of the money you spend on your credit card) to pay for the travel expenses. Earn enough travel points and cashback and it is possible to travel for free

Here are the steps to take and the tips to remember in order to travel for free using your credit card.

1. Apply for the right credit card.

This means that you will likely need a good credit score and if you don't have that, refer to our guide on how to achieve a good credit score. We also have a guide on how to climb the credit card ladder in the next chapter.

Go for a reward credit card with no cap as to the reward points you can earn. Ideally, the reward points should not have an expiration period, or at least have a longer expiration period. Keep an eye out for perks such as **complimentary companion tickets** and **waived baggage fees.**

There are generally two types of travel credit cards. **General purpose** credit cards give high rewards on all kinds of travel expenses, while **brand-specific** cards offer excellent rewards only when paying for the services of specific airlines or hotels. If you're loyal to a certain airway or hotel, you may want to choose the latter.

You'll probably have to pay an annual fee on the best travel rewards credit cards. Many cards don't have an annual fee in the first year, but starting in year two, you'll have to pay the fee. If you can earn enough rewards for a free flight or hotel, you'll hardly notice that you've paid the annual fee. If you do end up having to pay fees, make sure you pay them off right away, so you don't pay any interest on the annual fee.

2. Charge everything to your card.

Here's how you can get as many rewards points as possible – pay for everything with your card, including your groceries and other expenses – even utilities. Use it as much as you can. This doesn't mean that you should spend more than you can. In fact, you should only spend within your means. It only means that whenever you have to pay for something, use your cards.

3. Meet the minimum spending requirement

This is why the first tip is important. Some of the best rewards cards have minimum spending requirements. The Chase Sapphire Preferred card, for example, requires that you charge at least $3000 during the first 3 months!

Now, for many people, spending $3000 in three months just to get free flights just isn't feasible. The good news is that it's not as difficult as it looks. You can use your credit card to pay for a lot of things including utilities, taxes, and several months' worth of your insurance premiums in advance. You can buy gift cards at Amazon and then "sell" them to friends or use them further down the line.

You can even ask the company you work for if you can use your personal credit card for business expenses and then just have them reimburse you. You can also tell trustworthy friends and family that if they're looking to buy things, you'd appreciate if they'd use your card and then just reimburse you.

3. Join many rewards and frequent flyers programs

You can also enrol in airline and hotel loyalty programs. These will also pay rewards for your flights and stays. Enrolling is free. You just have to remember to use your loyalty program number when you book and charge to your credit card for more reward points.

They won't cost anything except perhaps a few minutes of your time. This doesn't mean you should scour the web for all rewards programs and sign up for every single one.

Start with your favorite service providers and if you have little travel experience, then start with what you're planning on your trip. Before you even book a flight and hotel rooms in your target destination, join the rewards programs of brands you're looking to spend for.

4. Enjoy your signup bonus

Find out if the credit card you applied for comes with a great sign up bonus. Collecting the bonus can be as easy as using the card to make a purchase within the first 3 months or paying the annual fee. It's a really good deal if the sign up bonus is higher than the annual fee.

5. Always pay your balance in full

This is one of the most crucial rules to follow when you're using any type of rewards credit card, especially when you are using a travel rewards card.

Paying your balance in full each month can help you increase your credit score. This will allow you to measure up for better credit card offers. Having a good credit score is crucial, but that's not the only reason to pay your balance in full each month.

It is important to pay finance charges on time since it cancels out the rewards obtained on the credit card. This happens when you carry a balance on your credit card beyond the time frame for payment.

6. Redeem your rewards right away

You can either use your rewards to book travel via the card's online booking tool, or you can redeem your rewards for a statement credit to reduce the amount that you owe. If you choose the statement credit option, you'll have to charge the expense of the travel to your credit card, and then, you have to use your rewards to credit the account for the travel expenses.

If you don't want to end up paying off the balance, exchange your rewards right away. Otherwise, you might have to pay at least the minimum payment to keep your account in good standing while you wait for the statement credit to post to your account.

7. Pay on time to avoid forfeiting your rewards

The fine print of your rewards credit card includes the things that can make you lose your credit card rewards. Most commonly, late payments can cost you all the points you've collected. It is the last thing you want after you've worked so hard to collect rewards.

3. Student credit cards

Card issuers market student credit cards to students and to people who have not yet owned a credit card. Student credit cards allow new users to establish a good credit history. It can help them in securing a car loan or an apartment in the future.

Pros

- Available for those with no credit score
- Easy to apply for
- No cash deposits required

Cons

- Interest rates can be high
- Low credit limit

4. Charge cards

Charge cards have no interest. But these types of payment cards require you to pay your balance fully every month. An uncapped credit limit is a feature of charge cards. In addition to that, charge cards come with generous rewards and benefits. However, their annual fee is high. It can range from $120 to $550.

This kind of credit card is best for high-income people.

Pros

- May allow unlimited spending
- You can acquire purchase points
- You can obtain points on travel and dining expenses
- Generous rewards
- It's flexible

Cons

- Missed payments can affect your credit score tremendously
- Need to pay in fully per month

5. Secured credit cards

Secured credit cards are credit cards that the cardholder guarantees with a safety deposit which is often tantamount to the entire line of credit. These cards usually have a controlled line of credit and come with an annual fee. After continual, responsible use, the issuer will return the security deposit. These cards may likewise be known as paid credit cards and semi-secured credit cards.

This kind of credit card is best for those with no or poor credit history.

Pros

- Available for credit newbies
- It can help you re-establish your credit scores
- Earn interest on your deposits
- Issuers report to credit bureaus

Cons

- The need for cash deposits

6. Sub-prime credit cards

A person with a sub-prime credit has a credit record that is too weak to be given rewards. Typically, sub-prime credit cards have high-interest rates. They also come with low credit limits and extra fees. This type of credit card is ideal for new users and individuals with a credit score of less than 600.

Pros

- Available for credit newbies
- Easy to apply for

Cons

- Unsecured
- With cash deposits

7. Prepaid cards

Prepaid cards are related to secured credit cards, but such cards are not linked to any bank account. In general, when you utilize a prepaid credit card, you are spending money that you have loaded onto the card. This is ideal for those who'd like to do some online shopping and those who want a convenient option to pay for travel deals.

Pros

- Available for consumers with damaged credit

- Available for credit newbies

Cons

- Require security deposits

- Have high percentage rates

- Does not help build credit score

- Has application fees

- With cash deposits

8. Limited purpose cards

Limited purpose cards are credit cards that can be used at a store or in fast-food chains. Limited purpose credit cards are accessible so it's ideal for new users, people who own small businesses who need supplies, shoppers, travelers, and sub-prime users.

Pros

- Available for credit newbies

- Freebies

- No need for security deposit

Cons

- With cash deposits

- Not flexible

9. Business credit cards

Business credit cards are designed to cover business expenses. They are not made for personal use. They help businesses in building a credit profile. This is for the purpose of improving future credit borrowing terms. They're discussed in detail in Chapter 10.

Pros

- Easy access to a revolving LOC

- Quickly access financing for short-term needs

- Increase the purchasing power of your company

Cons

- Has high-interest charges

- Limited balance

Basic Features of Credit Cards

Every credit card these days come with the following:

- **Purchase Rate**

  This is the interest rate that is applied to the charges you've made to your credit card. Note that this only applies to the balances that you were unable to pay in full by the end of your billing cycle that is already outside of the grace period. In the next section, you'll know more about this.

- **Credit limit**

  The issuer determines the credit limit set on the credit card. There are two types of credit limit.

  Normal credit limit is the usual credit provided by the lending institution during the issuance of the credit card.

  The revolving credit limit depends on how the card is used and on what items or services are purchased or availed.

- **Can be used to pay in foreign and domestic currency**

  Credit cards give you the ability to pay for goods and services in either domestic or foreign currency. With this feature, you can pay merchants in any part of the world.

- **All transactions are recorded**

  Lending institutions, like NBFCs or banks, record all of their credit card holder's transactions. The records help the entities to bill their credit card holders appropriately.

- **Service Fees**

  In the course of owning a credit card, you will encounter different kinds of credit card fees. These include balance transfer fees, one time processing fee, and credit limit increase fees.

  To know more about these, take a close look at your credit card agreement.

- **Regular charges**

  Issuers charge basic charges routinely as opposed to service fees that only occur when certain circumstances arise. Regular fees are nominal in nature, and there are two types of them: Annual charges and Additional charges. The latter are collected for supplementary services such as the issue of a new credit card.

- **Grace period**

  As mentioned before, the grace period is the period in which you won't incur financial and interest charges while carrying a balance. It's basically the amount of time you have before your new purchases start incurring charges. In the US, regulations dictate that consumers be given at least 21 days to pay before their purchase start incurring interest. You can find the length of your grace period on the back or front of your billing statement.

- **Service tax**

  This is always included in the amount charged to the borrower. The service tax is mandatory. Because of this, the final end cost paid by the user increases. Many issuing entities set policies that reverse the service tax that is charged on fuel, gas, and goods purchases.

- **Gifts, bonus points, and other offers**

  Conventionally, offering incentives is a trendy way to improve sales. Credit card providers also use this tactic when they market their credit cards. Therefore, card providers often give rewards, gifts, and bonus points to their cardholders. By accumulating bonus points, you can redeem cash back offers, gifts, and other rewards. To be eligible for many rewards, you may have to use your credit card frequently.

Factors to Consider When Choosing a Credit Card

A credit card is a handy tool for many occasions. However, it can inflict terrible damage to your life, budget, and monthly salary if you misuse it or choose the wrong type.

Not all credit cards are created equal. Here are some of the things you need to check when looking for a credit card

1. Interest rates

The Annual Percentage Rate is the interest rate that you have to pay yearly. The APR is an important factor to consider in comparing credit cards.

To compute the APR, multiply the monthly rate by twelve. The product, at times, is not what it appears to be. There are also introductory rates, which are also known as teaser rates. They are considered as interest rates that are charged to a client during the initial stages of a loan.

Depending on the financial institution, the teaser rate can be as low as 0%. It's not permanent and it expires after a specific period of time. The value of the rate depends on the card's balance.

Other than teaser rates, there are other types of rates that apply to transactions made using the card. The rates depend on the type of transaction and on how the cardholder uses his or her credit card. For example, cash advances have high-interest rates, and apart from the APR, other rates apply to balance transfers.

You have to check the clauses on the agreement regarding the card's APR in order to know whether the deal is good in the long term or not. People often read the short term deals only. They fail to check the other provisos included in a contract. For your best interest, you must read everything carefully.

Furthermore, APRs are either variable or fixed. This means that they either depend on the prime rate or remain constant. The prime rate is the interest rate that issuers lend to their prime customers – the most creditworthy ones. Variable-rate credit cards are pegged to the prime rate. The APR of variable-rate credit cards can change. It is usually tied to an index.

Being a benchmark rate, an index is considered as the LIBOR or the prime rate. For instance, if it is stated in the agreement that the APR is prime plus 10% and the benchmark rate is at 5%, the credit card's interest rate is 15%.

As a further matter, you have to understand what the lending institution will charge you aside from the prime rate and whether the company can change the rate or not.

2. Grace period or billing cycle

The billing cycle determines when you should start paying interest on the purchases that you make using your credit card. It's advised to choose a credit card that offers a long grace period.

3. Fees

Most credit cards have annual fees. Annual fees are not always that bad, especially if you are paying the annual fee to acquire something that can benefit you. For example, some credit cards offer a lot of miles or travel points even though their annual fee is higher than others. Flyer miles are part of an airline or a financial institution's loyalty program.

When choosing from different types of credit cards, be sure to check their fees and to see the rewards you can get from the credit cards with high annual fees. Also, if there is no fee, check the APR. It can be higher than others. Furthermore, transferring your balance to another payment card or taking cash advances can also make you incur additional fees.

4. Expiry dates and special offers

Some lending companies offer special APR, cash advance rates, and balance transfer fees. You have to make sure to check the expiry dates of these offers.

In every credit card agreement, the APR is presented as a certain percentage. If you see an asterisk or any sign beside the APR, you must thoroughly read the fine print.

5. Penalties and Minimums

Lenders require users to pay a minimum portion of the debt every month. It can either be a flat fee or a percentage. If you don't pay the monthly fee before the due date, the company will charge you with a penalty fee. If it will be hard for you to pay a fixed amount per month, choose the credit card that has no non-payment fee or the one that offers the lowest limit.

6. Rewards and Points

Most credit cards offer rewards and points for utilizing them. Excellent rewards often come with a fee. There are no-fee credit cards that offer rewards and points too. Once you've chosen a credit card that offers the best deals on fees, grace period, and interest rates, check the rewards and points that you can get.

7. Specialization

Some credit cards are designed for shoppers, travelers, business people, students etc. Thus, you must choose the type that is right for your needs. For example, the credit cards tailored for students have low spending limits and low fees.

In a similar way, credit cards that are designed for wealthy consumers have low APR but the credit limit is high. Cards designed for travelers offer redeemable points for flights and other bonus points, but its annual fee may be high.

8. Credit limit

The credit limit of your chosen type of credit card must cover your needs. The amount must be enough to provide flexibility, but it must not be higher than what you can afford to pay.

Low-limit cards are perfect for college students, whereas high limit cards are tailored for business people and wealthy folks. Remember that spending a low percentage of your credit limit per month is one of the best ways to increase your credit score.

Whether you want to upgrade your credit card or you are applying to get one for the first time, keep those factors in mind.

Ways to Avoid a Finance Charge on Your Credit Card

Finance charges are calculated based on recent purchases and unpaid balance so when you're late in paying the minimum monthly payment, you will incur finance charges. A finance charge is compensation to the lending institution for extending credit or for providing the funds to a borrower.

The single most effective way to avoid finance charges is to pay your balance on time. Don't settle for paying the minimum. Note that finance charges are used by card issuers to charge their customers for carrying a balance, so the best way to avoid them is to refrain from carrying a balance in the first place. Paying your balance fully before the end of every billing cycle prevents you from incurring finance charges.

Remember that every credit card has a grace period. Typically, it is between 21 and 25 days. During the grace period, you do not incur finance charges. So to pay zero finance charges, pay your credit balance fully during the grace period.

You may also transfer your balance to another card to dodge additional charges. This is recommended if you can't pay your balance in full within the grace period. Consider transferring your balance to another card with low APR. For instance, some credit cards give you zero percent APR for a specific period.

By transferring your credits, you can, in a way, get rid of your balance cheaply. However, keep in mind that you can't do that forever. Transferring your balance may also come with fees plus you will still have to pay for that amount in the credit card you transferred it to.

Finally, be wary of promos. When the 0% APR promo expires, you are obliged to pay a higher interest rate than before, so be sure to read and complete the terms and conditions of the agreement.

There is a database in which you can read and check out all the different credit card agreements available from various companies online. It's available on the site of the Consumer Financial Protection Bureau. You can check the list out at www.consumerfinance.gov. Do your research and you'll be spared from a lot of headache.

Did You Know?

The FICO score is based on the behavior of millions of borrowers. The model looks for patterns in behavior that indicates a borrower might default, as well as patterns that indicated a borrower is likely to pay.

Chapter 9

How To Climb The Credit Card Ladder

Credit cards are a good way to build or repair credit scores and as you get better scores, you'll find yourself being able to apply for better cards.

You'll start from the basic cards with no benefits and eventually get to enjoy credit cards with amazing cash back offers. You might even end up with prestigious cards that reward you with international lounge access. Or if you are an extremely high earner, you can avail of invite only cards available to the wealthy.

Each credit card tier has corresponding credit score and income requirements. You do not have to aspire for the most premium card. The card you choose to start with and then upgrade to should suit your long-term needs and your income status at the time.

Tier 1

This is where you'll find the starter cards. Those who are beginning to build their credit score or improving it are recommended to start with these cards. These are great for students, people with bad credit score, and immigrants just started settling in US. Some of Tier 1 credit cards have annual fees. There are also no rewards, cashback, and airline miles.

Student cards

Students can start using credit card and begin to establish credit score. After some time, the feature of these cards can include cashback and rewards program. Generally, you should be a student to be eligible to avail this card.

Basic or secured cards

This is a no-frills credit card. Non-students should apply for a secured card. Like the students cards, this can also level up to cards with more useful features.

Interestingly, Discover is the only major credit card issuer that offers cashback for secured cards. But Discover is not honored at every establishment. In the event that your Discover card is declined, pay with a debit card. Also, you should not prioritize spending yet because the goal is to build credit and not earn points.

You should not concern yourself with interest rates and late fees either because you are expected to pay your balances in time and in full. Also, the credit limit should not matter because you are supposed to build your credit and not rely on the card often. But to be exact, the credit limit on these cards is based on the minimum or maximum deposits.

Secured cards require minimum deposits in case you are not able to pay the monthly bills. Capital One has the lowest minimum deposit at $49. Bank of America, US Bank, and Wells Fargo have the highest minimum deposit of $300. As for maximum deposit, it ranges from $2500 to $10000.

Not all secured credit cards have annual fees. Citi, Discover, and Capital One do not require annual fees. Wells Fargo, Bank of America and US Bank have annual fees of $25, $39, and $25, respectively.

If the card issuer upgrades the card to unsecured credit card, they might still charge annual fees. But you can talk to them about waiving the fee. One tip is to insinuate that you might close your accounts if you still have to pay the annual fee.

Product change is swapping a credit card to other cards in the issuer's portfolio. You can do this when you upgrade to an unsecured credit card. Bank of America requires that you deposited a considerable sum in their bank to access the valuable cards, otherwise, other card issuers have better choices. Capital One's best unsecured card may be the Quicksilver card that earns 1.5% on all purchases.

Citi has Costco card, Citi Double Cash card, and the Citi Dividend card that offer more than 2% cashback. US Bank has the US Bank Cash Card+ as the best option for cashback reward. Wells Fargo has an inconvenient inquiry process for product change. You may be better off choosing from the other issuers.

Subprime cards

If you do not qualify for the student and secured credit cards, you can opt to apply for a subprime card. However, these are not very practical because they incur high fees. They have a monthly fee but no benefits to speak of. Subprime cards should be your last resort.

You might be tempted to get these because of very little requirements and that there's no deposit needed. However, they are not valuable and will be costly to keep in the long run.

Whichever tier 1 credit card you choose, it is advisable to keep using the card for 6 to 12 months before upgrading to a higher level one. Keep in mind that you are building or improving your credit score. Practice responsible use of these cards. You should have accumulated a credit score of more than 650 before moving on the next tier.

A technique you can use to increase our credit score is to prepay your cards. Do not max them out but leave a small balance to decrease utilization. Of course, you should pay the full balance after the statement closes.

Tier 2

When you finally graduate to a higher tier card, these can further establish the foundation of your credit score. You can now begin earning rewards by optimizing points. You can get reward points or cash back with your purchases. These cards also offer sign up bonuses.

One of the most common kinds is the travel rewards card. But be careful with this because it's pointless to optimize for free travel or other rewards by accruing tons of debt.

The credit limit on these cards ranges from $500 to $10000. In order to avail one, you have to have a credit score of 690 to 720. You will be also asked to provide a proof of income.

Cashback cards are some of the more common cards under this category. With these cards, you get a small amount of money back by charging purchases to your credit card, hence the name. You redeem it by deducting your cashback from the statement balance, deposit in a bank account, or redeem as gift cards.

Cashback comes in different modes: flat percentage, bonus category, and tiered rewards. Flat percentage cashback credit cards earn the same rebate with every spending. It appeals to the busy, straightforward consumers. Bonus category and tiered reward cards entail strategic purchasing but earn bigger cashback. These are for people who do not mind planning their spending to get more cashback.

Cashback rewards overweigh the banks interest rate. For example, with a low bank interest rate, you can only earn 0.6% annual yield with a usual savings account. You will earn better returns with at least 1% cashback on purchases. Cashback is also tax-free.

Travel benefits are other main rewards on higher tier credit cards. You can travel for free if you save enough points to redeem rewards. Use your credit card on all travel-related purchases. You also have to pay your full balance every month. That way, there will be no interest fee and no late fees to pay off. Plus, you may lose your saved points if you are late in paying your balances.

Tier 2 Cards Worth Taking a Look At

If you want to save travel points, Chase has the best travel cards available. You can start with their cards. However, Chase has a 5/24 rule. If you apply for one of their cards, you will be rejected if you have 5 new cards in your credit report for the past 24 months.

Chase Freedom credit cards

These cards can accumulate Ultimate Rewards (UR) which is transferrable to a higher tier Chase card to optimize reward redemption. Chase Freedom has a $150 sign up bonus after spending $500 in 3 months. It also has a 5% cashback on various categories that change every quarter. Cashback is applicable up to $1500 in combined spending. It requires activation every quarter.

Chase Freedom Unlimited

This one has the same sign up bonus but offers 1.5% cashback on all purchases. Both credit cards offer sign up bonus of 15,000 UR points. If you get a higher level card, the Chase Sapphire Reserve for instance, you will a get better optimization of reward points upon redemption.

Discover It

This has 5% cashback on changing categories each quarter, up to $1500 value of combined purchases. It has cashback match of 10% in the first year. The card also offers attractive Discover Deals where you can use the cashback match. However, there are a few cons for the issuer, like Discover removing long term insurance options for their credit cards. This means, Discover cards would not be recommended if you intend on long-standing warranty or return protection for long term purchases.

Discover It Miles

On the other hand, this card offers 1.5% cashback on every purchase, 3% cashback match for the first year which is usable on Discover Deals.

US Bank Cash+ credit card

This one has cashback offer with the added perk of being able to choose the rotating categories each quarter. The card offers 5% cashback on 2 chosen categories, until $2000 in combined spending. It also has 2% cashback on everyday purchase category such as groceries, gas, or restaurants, and 1% cash back on other purchases.

The American Express Blue Cash Everyday

With this card, you can enjoy a 3% cashback on grocery store purchases, maximum of $6000 worth of spending. It also has 2% cashback at gas station spending and selected department stores, and 1% cashback on anything else. This card earns cash back through statement credits.

Amex Everyday

This one has Membership Reward (MR) Points. It earns twice the MR points at grocery stores up to $6000 on combined purchases. It also offers 1x MR points anywhere else. if you reached more than 20 transactions per billing, you also earn 20% bonus in MR points. If you want to earn travel rewards and availing an Amex Platinum or Amex PRG soon, it is recommended you go for the Amex Everyday card.

Citi Double Cash card

If you want to eliminate having to deal with changing categories and thinking of which card to choose, you may opt for Citi Double Cash card. It offers 2% cashback on every purchase. You can also earn an additional 1% cashback when you pay the balance of said purchases. You can redeem cashback as a check, gift card, or statement credit.

Citi Bank cards offer perks such as Return Guarantee and Price Protection. They also have Citi Private Pass which can be valuable in availing Citi's presale or exclusive passes. It covers the best in dining, live music, family entertainment, dining, among others.

Choosing and using a Tier 2 Card

Choose a card with no annual fees. Any card issuer should be glad to have your business especially since at this point, you have proven that you are a responsible cardholder.

Remember to keep paying your balances in full every time to avoid interest payment and to maintain good credit.

Avoid cash advances and balance transfers. They incur extra charges and do not give you any rewards. These also lessen the available credit you can use towards earning rewards.

Take advantage of the sign up bonus, there are great ones like free flight. You have to spend a set amount on the card within the first three months of getting it. Pick a card with a sign up bonus that is easy to redeem. The minimum purchase should be manageable for you to pay off each month.

Take note that when you upgrade to tier 3 card, you should still keep your tier 2 card. They are now called anchor cards. These increase your score in the long run. It is better if the tier 2 card has no annual fee. Just make sure to charge purchases on it every 5 months to keep it active.

Tier 3

These credit cards have better benefits than tier 2 cards. They may have annual fees or not. If carrying an annual fee, the value of rewards should be greater than the annual fee. Most of its perks are travel-related. It also has a more attractive sign up bonus.

Annual fees of tier 3 cards are priced at $65 minimum. To get one of these cards, you should have a credit score ranging from 710 to 740. You also have to show that you are earning close to $61,000 per year while having a good credit history.

Because you get this card for the rewards, you have to compare its cost and benefits. For example, the Chase Hyatt card offers free overnight stay every year. This certainly outweighs the annual payment of $75.

When choosing a tier 3 card, you have to consider also the hidden cost along with the obvious cost. This is the same for main benefits and hidden benefits. You can think of the annual fees as the main cost and opportunity cost as the hidden cost. And sign up bonuses and points earned are the main benefits while improving the credit score criteria is a hidden benefit.

Cards carrying annual fees have sign up bonuses. You can also earn points on chosen categories that have purchase multipliers. The hidden benefit of using the card is the improvement of the credit score criteria such as number of accounts given that you pay the full balance in time monthly and also the average of accounts.

If you are after travel perks, a good option to consider may be Citi Prestige. It has an annual fee is $450 and a sign-up bonus of $250 in travel credit. The next thing to think about is can you get $200 worth or more from other benefits. The other rewards include Priority Pass, Global Entry or TSA Pre-check credit, 3-hour trip delay protection, and 4th night free hotel stay.

The 4th night free benefit can be used multiple times a year. You can get at least $200 worth just using this perk alone. For instance, you can plan to take four vacations of at least 4 days in one year. You have four nights free. Thinking in terms of cost, if the price is $100 per night, you can have $400 in savings. If the price is $200 a night, you can save $800.

If you want to optimize rewards and receive benefits worth more than the card costs, you have to spend a bit of time to think of the positive value of using the card. And what kind of benefits are you really looking after and will you be actually able to use the rewards. Only then, will keeping a rewards-heavy card be worth it.

Tier 4

For those who earn good income regularly, this is most prestigious card. Benefits include access to airport lounges around the world. These carry higher annual fees that range from $400 to $550. You can also add additional cardholders. Adding additional users means additional annual fees up to $175 each cardholder.

To be eligible for tier 4 credit cards, you should have a credit score of at least 730. If you have a score lower than 730, you should be earning $61,000 or more per year. Or you can have a lower income but you should have a good credit history and high score. You will get the most of these cards if you are a frequent flyer.

They also have higher spending multiplier than tier 3 credit cards. Chase Sapphire, for instance, earns 3 times on travel purchases. It also has $300 travel credit, $100 Global Entry/TSA Precheck Credit, and unlimited Priority Pass Access.

Not all cards have fees for additional cardholders. Hilton Amex Aspire, Delta Reserve Card, SPG Luxury Card, and United Club Card do not carry annual fees for additional users. Moreover, Hilton Amex Aspire offers $100 property credit for additional users that can used for 2-night stay at Conrad properties and Waldorf Astoria.

Amex Platinum has a sign-up bonus of 60,000 Membership Rewards (MR) points ($1140 value) which is redeemable after spending $5,000 in charged purchasing in the first 90 days. Hilton Amex Aspire offers $150,000 Hilton Honor (HH) points (worth $900) after spending $4000 in purchases during the first 90 days. Chase Sapphire Reserve has a sign-up bonus of $50,000 in Ultimate Rewards (UR) points (worth $1050) upon charging a $4000 worth of purchases in the first 3 months.

Amex Platinum earns 5 MR points per dollar spent on airfare-related purchases and prepaid hotel stays booked through the airline or Amex. There is 1 MR point for other spending. Hilton Amex Aspire offer 4 HH points per dollar spent on Hilton-owned properties internationally, 7 HH points per dollar spent on airline tickets booked through the airline or Amex, on car rentals booked directly with the participating companies, and purchases on US restaurants. They offer 3 HH points on other purchases. Chase Sapphire rewards has 3 UR points per dollar spent on dining and travel purchases, and 1 UR point for all other spending.

In choosing a Tier 4 card or cards, weigh the combination of rewards that would suit you best. Especially since the competition among these premium travel cards intensified with the enhanced benefits.

Tier 5

This is the invite-only credit card. Among these cards are the American Express Centurion and JPMorgan Chase Reserve. You are eligible for the JPMorgan Reserve if you have around $10 million managed by JPMorgan. To qualify for the American Express Centurion, you should have a $16 million net worth and yearly earnings of $1.3 million. Amex Centurion carries a $2500 annual fee and a $7500 signup fee.

These exclusive credit cards have lavish perks. For example, the American Centurion cardholders enjoy no credit limit, Membership Reward points, and exclusive upgrades and benefits to dining, travel, entertainment and more. The other benefits are still shrouded in mystery.

Another Tier 5 card, the Dubai First Royale Mastercard card comes with the services of a relationship manager that caters to the owner's specific whims. The manager also assists the cardholder book private getaways and vacations. This card is known as one of the most exclusive in the world. You have to be based in Dubai to have a chance of being invited.

Did You Know?

The minimum credit card payment is the LEAST amount you can pay to keep the card active. If you pay less, your card will be deactivated (turned off)

Congratulations!

The sixth character of the password required to unlock the Additional Funding Sources Booklet is letter n.

Chapter 10

Business Credit Cards

Whenever you attempt to open up a new business, you will need some funding to cover a lot of its initial expenses. Your personal credit card will be sufficient to start the business but only to a point. If the business you are planning to set up is of a certain size, you might want to apply for a business credit card.

What are business credit cards and what makes them different?

A business credit card shares mostly the same functions with a typical personal credit card. You use them to make transactions and pay for the charges each card makes at the end of the month. However, there are certain aspects that make a business credit card considerably different from your typical card.

1. It's Not Covered by Most Consumer Protection Laws

This is quite simple: under the law, businesses are of a different category from what you will call "consumers". Sure, you can tell yourself that you yourself are a consumer but the credit card was issued for the legal entity that makes up your business.

This means that certain consumer protection laws like the Credit Card Act of 2009 won't apply to you as the card holder. This could lead to a number of problems which will include sudden shifts in that card's Annual Percentage Rate, even overnight at some instances, and charges for penalties and fees that border on being expensive and unreasonable.

However, there is a silver lining to all of this. If your business is quite small, some consumer protection laws might be extended to you. This is not true for all issuers so it's best not to expect to be covered once you are issued the card.

2. It Affects All Credit, Both Business and Personal

When it comes to being a business owner, the distinction between your personal credit and the business's credit is often blurred. In other words, your personal credit can affect how the business itself can apply for and use credit.

For instance, when issuers look at your application for a business credit card, they would look at your personal information and check if you have what it takes to handle the kind of liabilities that their product entails. As such, poor financial management skills might affect your ability to secure a credit card for the business in the first place.

It also goes without saying that reporting your transactions to the reporting agencies can get mixed. For instance, you might get a credit report where your entries for both your personal and business transactions are made into your timeline. Of course, this means that any mark reported to that agency regarding your business credit card's transactions, whether good or bad, will affect your credit score.

3. Higher Credit Limits

Due to the fact that your business is going to make a lot of expenses, the starting credit limit for a business credit card tends to be higher compared to personal ones. As such, if you can expect your business to make a lot of notable transactions, it's best that you apply for a credit card for businesses so you don't max your cards out quickly.

Of course, the same things that affect your credit score as a private individual will also affect you as the business owner. Even with the higher credit limit, the system of credit utilization rates still apply. Any credit you have available on that card, then, will be compared to the credit that you actually use on a regular basis. Depending on the reporting agency, credit utilization may comprise 30% to 40% of your score.

If you are not the type to overly rely on your business credit card, this could be an advantage for you. The higher credit limit means that it will take several huge purchases for you to even reach the 30% threshold reporting agencies recommend credit card users stick to. So as long as your credit utilization is within 15% to 19%, your credit score should remain high.

4. Perks

Due to the fact that business cards are a bit more demanding to maintain, certain credit card issuers offer certain perks for those that do apply for such. The most common perks are discounts for payments of several utility services like electricity, Internet connection, and phone connection. Some issuers even provide discounts on Wi-Fi rates as well as office supplies which might be an advantage for businesses that rely a lot on these.

However, you might be more interested with flat-rate rewards programs where you can avail of certain bonuses every time you make a purchase with the card. It's best to consult with the issuer first before you submit your application so you know what rewards you can expect if you frequently use that card.

Personal vs. business: Which card should you choose?

As was stated, there is the option to use your personal credit card over a business credit card for most of your transactions. If you are still deciding whether to stick to your personal card or apply for a business card, there are certain factors that you should consider.

You might be better off with a business credit card if:

- You are a starting entrepreneur who wants to build your business's credit trustworthiness.
- You run a company whose expenses require a larger credit limit.
- Your expenses align most with reward categories that business cards offer.
- You no longer want to deal with low credit limits.

However, a personal credit card might be for you if:

- You run a sole proprietorship whose business expenses fall below the usual personal credit card limits.
- Your expenses do not align with the rewards program most business credit cards offer.

- You are not interested in building credit for the business.
- You are not the one who would apply for a business loan anytime in the future.

Who can apply for a business credit card?

Naturally, the first requirement you need to qualify for a business card is to have a business. So, if you don't have at least any form of business, does that mean that you are not qualified for a business credit card?

The answer, surprisingly, is no. You can actually qualify for a business credit card even if you are just interested in the rewards that these cards have.

The reason for this is quite simple: there is no strict definition as to what a "business" actually is. It could range from hawking wares at a flea market or running a corporation with a hundred employees in it. It doesn't even matter if your previous business experience involves setting up a lemonade stand outside your home.

So as long as the money you generated from your activities can be considered as business revenue, then you might find some use for a business credit card. Either way, the issuer will still look at your personal credit information to see if you have what it takes to meet the demands that the card entails.

Types of Business Cards

There are several business cards that you can apply for. They have the same functions and requirements but they will carry certain features that make them ideal in a number of situations. They are as follows:

1. Business Credit Cards

These are your typical credit card and they function mostly the same with a personal card. They have a credit limit that dictates how much you can use the card every month as well as how much you pay.

Whenever your card makes a charge, you are obligated to pay the charge each billing cycle. This doesn't mean you have to immediately pay the amount in full as you can pay in installments. Although, this does mean that you carry the balance month for month i.e. you will have to deal with interest rates until that debt is settled.

However, this does allow for a small financial cushion that small business owners can depend on during tough times.

2. Business Charge Cards

Like the typical business card, charge cards have the same function as personal credit cards. However, they differ greatly in the aspect of credit limits since, basically, there is none.

Charge cards have something that is called as a "shadow" limit which tend to be higher than most credit card limits and can be flexible depending on the card holder's needs. They can also change depending on how often you use your card as well as the overall status of your credit history.

However, there is a catch: Going over the limit can cause your account to be frozen. Also, you can never carry your balance on a month to month basis. You'll have to pay the charge in full every billing period.

This card is recommended only for people who have full control over their spending habits. If you can spend only on what you can afford, this charge card might be ideal for you.

3. Secure Business Cards

This card is ideal for businesses with little personal credit or none at all. Think of it as a credit builder card, only for business owners.

How it works is quite simple. When you apply for this card, you are required to deposit a minimum amount. This could be in between $2,000.00 and $5,000.00, depending on the card and the issuer.

This amount serves as your credit line and you can use that to pay for anything related to the business. Either way, every payment for that balance will be reported by the issuer to the credit reporting agency.

This way, your business can build up on its credit within a year. However, it's important to note that only on-time payments will be reported. Any payment you miss will be a derogatory mark, defeating the purpose of the card.

How to get a business credit card

The process of securing your business's credit card is surprisingly easy. In fact, the process is quite similar to getting a personal credit card. However, there are differences in the details that you will submit to the issuing company. Since this is a business credit card, then it would be apparent that the issuer would ask information regarding your business.

The application form will include questions like:

- The legal name of the business
- Address
- The type of industry it belongs to. Some industries are considered high-risk and high-maintenance which could affect the approval of your application.
- The structure of the company whether you are a sole proprietorship, a partnership, or a corporation.
- The age of the business i.e. how long it has been operating.
- Number of people employed as well as the organizational structure.
- Annual revenue
- Estimated monthly expenditures and other finance-related matters.

It really depends on the institution as to what kind of information that they want from you. To make it easier on your part, it's best to look for the information on your part and prepare your documents and answers beforehand.

What you need to secure a quick approval

In the end, it is up to the discretion of the bank or any similar financial institution to decide whether or not to approve your application for a business credit card. To make them easily decide for your approval, there are a few things you have to do beforehand:

1. Have a Business

Although you don't exactly have to have a business to qualify for a business credit card, having one does tend to improve your odds of successfully securing one. The lending institution would most likely want to make sure that whatever credit or money you can secure through the card would be used to invest for an actual venture. One proof that you have a business is through securing an Employer's Identification Number from the Internal Revenue Service as well as opening a business account.

2. Have a Good to Excellent Personal Credit Score

Your personal credit score will actually influence how your application is going to be treated. That lender would have to make sure that you as the applicant have what it takes to meet the demands of the card.

For this, they would pull up a hard search on your personal credit history and look for any mark made regarding your financial activities. What one creditor would look for is different from another but it's safe to say that applicants with a history of on-time payments, good credit utilization rates, and minimal to no derogatory marks tend to have a better chance of getting their applications approved.

What transactions could the business credit card be used for?

There is actually no hard and fast rule as to where and how you should use your business's credit card. It has the same functions as your typical credit card albeit with a larger credit limit and a few more restrictions/obligations on your part.

The question, then, is not on where your business credit card will be the most applicable but on how to optimize its usage while minimizing the risks it entails. To do those, here are a few tips to keep in mind.

1. Keep Everything Strictly Within Business

Even if you are running a sole proprietorship, resist any urge to use that card to spend for personal concerns. Keeping your business expenses separate from your personal one is one way to keep track of your expenses and claim deductions when taxing season comes around.

If you authorize your employees to use the card also, give guidelines as to what will qualify as a business expense. Having a system set up where employees have to seek approval before using the card and furnish receipts is a good way of enforcing accountability and limiting the card's use.

2. Make a Policy

If you are running a corporation, chances are your partners will also want to have access to that card. This would be an opportunity for you to draft a policy on how to use that card.

Make it a point to show to everyone that the card is accessible but only if they meet certain conditions and follow the guidelines. The point here is to be as transparent as possible in telling your staff and your partners who can use the card and for what purposes.

3. Set Limits

The 30% rule for personal credit card utilization rates apply here as well. If possible, do not go beyond 30% of the available credit when using the card. If the limit is at $10,000.00, then your spending should not be over $3,000.00.

Of course, there is a chance when the policy you have set up would not work in all situations. Some authorized users for the card might have different purposes in mind for it. This is where a bit of creativity comes into play.

You might set different limits for each user but you must set other limiters as well. For example, one user might only access the card for a certain set of situations or you rotate possession of the card to the different users on a bi-weekly basis. The point is to make sure that nobody gets to use the card for too long to avoid abuses.

Did You Know?

If you pay your bill in full during the grace period, you won't have to pay a finance charge on purchases for that bill. A grace period is usually about 25 days.

Chapter 11

Credit Card Balance Transfer

Most people have been in that situation wherein expenses are suddenly crashing down on them all at the same time. To ease the cash flow, they turn to their credit cards for help. Before they knew it, they have maxed out the credit limit and are in even deeper trouble than they were before. But there might be a way to get out of this mess, and that is by taking advantage of credit card balance transfers.

Balance Transfer in a Nutshell

By the name itself, balance transfer is moving all of your outstanding balances from one or more of your credit card accounts to a new one with lower interest rates, fewer penalties, and more perks. Its main benefit is that you will be able to pay off the debt in fixed, monthly amounts with significantly reduced interest. It's very similar to paying a loan.

Through this option, you can save hundreds of dollars by simply moving all your credit card balances into a new credit card so you can manage your debt better. This works well if you're paying for a card that's almost maxed out, paying multiple credit cards at the same time, or just want to clear off your bills.

The interest rates depend on the length of the payment contract which can range from 6% up to 18.79% per year. So before you proceed with the transfer, you should compare rates and also ask for hidden fees required for the transfer especially if the credit card is from a different bank.

When Should You Do a Balance Transfer?

There are a couple of things you should consider before doing a credit card balance transfer.

First, you need to be absolutely committed to getting out of your credit card debt once and for all.

Since the balance transfer contract means you'll have to allot monthly amounts to pay off the loan. This will cut through your budget and you might just end up using your credit cards again. After all, it's easy to be tempted to use a zero balance credit card. To minimize the likelihood, you should reduce the number of cards you have. Start with those with annual fees and fewer perks. Although keeping card lines open makes your credit score healthy, the records for a closed credit card remains viable up to 10 years after the contract was terminated, so you should be good.

Second, you need to know your credit standing before you apply for a new card offering the balance transfer.

How extensive is your credit history? Longer is better, by the way. Have you ever been late for payment for more than 30 days? Are you almost maxed out on all your credit cards? You'll have a better chance of getting approved for a balance transfer if your total credit card debt is below 50% of your credit cards' combined limit. This is referred to as the utilization ratio. Also, if your credit score is more than 720, you should be good to go. There will be approval doubts if you're between 660 and 720. Anything lower than 660 reduces the chances of getting a balance transfer approved significantly.

Pros and Cons of Balance Transfer

Pros

- Lower interest rates. This is the balance transfer's biggest draw, which is actually good especially if your current credit card has an insanely high interest rate. Lower interest rates mean you can reduce your credit balance card in less time.
- Better terms. Short grace period and high fees are just some of the terms your current credit card has committed you into. Your new credit card, however, may have better offerings aside from the balance transfer option like a better rewards system.
- Debt consolidation. If this new credit card has a high enough limit, you can transfer all your balances to this new account and get rid of the others. This way, you'll be able to manage your debt easier and you don't have to make separate payments to different banks.

Cons

- Higher interest rates. This usually happens if you're not qualified for the promotional interest rates. Qualifications were mentioned in the previous section. Basically, you need a good enough credit score to make the cut. Otherwise, you're stuck with the regular interest rates.
- Can get expensive. If the new credit card has annual fees and you also need to pay a balance transfer fee, you might end up paying more than working it out with your current credit card debts. Consider these amounts before you commit into balance transfer.
- More debt risks. Making sure that you don't get tempted to use your credit cards once you've cleared off the balances is a practice in discipline. That's because you have more credit available at your disposal. This can be good or bad depending on how you manage your finances.

Balance transfer may be worth it if, in the end, you'll be saving money and paying off your credit card balances. There are drawbacks and not all are entitled to this option.

Did You Know?

When you use your credit card, you're borrowing money. So you will be charged interest whenever you don't pay your bill in full. With a credit card, you are paying for convenience. Credit card rates can be 18% or as high as 24% depending on your credit history.

Chapter 12

How to Protect Your Credit Card from Identity Theft

Identity theft is an existing crisis in the US that's continuing to grow every year. An Identity Theft Resource Center (ITRC) report is quite disturbing. It shows that 1,579 data breaches exposed about 179 million identity records in 2017.

Being a victim of an identity scam can cause you a lot of problems. One of the worst cases would be the downfall of your credit score.

How identity theft can ruin your credit score

The most common type of identity theft crime is credit card fraud. Fraudsters would steal your personal information and your credit card details. They would then use the stolen information for unauthorized transactions.

The fraudsters can either steal your credit card or perform a card-not-present fraud. But, they'd also need information such as your birthday and Social Security number.

You may end up with a credit card bill that you might not be able to pay or handle if you become a victim. This may affect your credit score if you don't act on it fast.

Ways to avoid becoming an identity theft victim

Proving that you're a victim of identity theft can be inconvenient. There's a long process to go through which involves a lot of documentation before you can prove your innocence.

It would still be best to avoid these kinds of troubles and there are several ways you can do it.

1. Watch out for Phishing Scams

A phishing scam is a criminal's method to get personal information such as passwords. The most common way of phishing is sent via e-mail.

These e-mails would look like official e-mails from a bank or other companies. The contents would often inform you about system changes or promotional offers. It would ask you to enter personal information because of these reasons. In some cases, these emails scare you into providing info by saying that that access to your account will be restricted if you don't "update" your account.

The e-mail would also contain an external link to a fraud web page that would look like the bank's legit website. Entering your personal details on this page will result in big problems for you. The criminals will use your details to perform transactions under your name.

You can avoid being a victim by remembering one important rule: Banks generally will never ask for your information. If you absolutely have to make sure you need to update your account, contact your bank first.

To avoid these scams, stay updated with the latest phishing scam techniques. An updated browser and firewalls also help to prevent phishing scams.

There are also anti-phishing toolbars available online. These will alert you if you visit a suspicious website.

2. Protect your computer data

Defrauders can also get vital information about you by hacking your personal computer.

They can use a keylogger that records everything you type on your computer. They may also intercept your Internet traffic and record information you send online.

People who transact online are the most vulnerable to these kinds of attacks. But, there are various ways to safeguard your computer data from hackers.

You must use a firewall and set a password for your WiFi. You should also install reliable anti-malware software. Many hackers use malware and other viruses to get information from computers.

Also, make sure that you're using secured connections. Public WiFi connections aren't secured, so it's best to avoid using them as much as possible.

3. Protect your passwords

Using passwords is one of the ways that keep accounts safe. But, not using them properly would still make you vulnerable to identity theft.

Your password must be strong and not guessable. Shocking as it may seem, many people use "password" and "123456" as their passwords. These are actually the weakest passwords anybody could use.

Avoid using birthdays, phone numbers, or other personal information as your password. It's best to use a combination of numbers, letters, and symbols. In this way, your password will be difficult to crack.

However, highly-skilled hackers may still be able to get your password. Using multifactor authentication especially for online banking might add security to your accounts. Some banks, for example, require that you confirm a transaction by using a temporary pin sent to your registered phone number.

You must also have different passwords for different accounts. If one of your accounts gets hacked, all your other accounts would likely be vulnerable as well.

The most important thing to remember is to never share your passwords with anybody.

4. Protect your mail

Imagine all the information an identity thief could get from your mailbox.

Criminals do not only steal information online. They can also get your personal information from the mail you receive if they find a chance.

To avoid mail identity theft, start by cutting down the amount of junk mail you receive. This includes insurance and credit offers.

You should also keep mail with important information in a locked container. If your mail is piling up, you can shred them instead.

For incoming mail, you can either get a locking mailbox or a P.O. Box. The locking mailbox looks like a normal mailbox, but it can only be opened with a key. A P.O. Box may be safer than a locking mailbox, but you'll need to pay for it monthly.

For outgoing mail, you must avoid putting it in a mailbox especially if it contains checks or cash. Instead, drop it off at the post office or in a collection box. You may also hand it directly to a mail carrier.

But with today's technology, companies now offer paperless bills. This will not only prevent mail fraud, but you may also get some small bill discounts.

5. Protect your credit card number

As mentioned above, fraudsters can use your credit card to perform unauthorized purchases. All they need is your credit card number and your personal information.

The basics of securing your credit card start with your signature. Sign the back of your credit card as soon as you get it. Also, don't write and keep your pin in the same place where your card is.

Keep your credit card safe by not letting anyone in public see it. Sometimes, you may receive calls from your "bank". Unless you made the call, never give your card information.

You must also watch out for phishing scam e-mails from your bank. Even if it looks legit, don't give your personal details or credit card number.

It's also a good idea to update your bank information regularly. Update your phone numbers and e-mail address as soon as changes occur. Also, be up-to-date with fraud alert systems and respond immediately to notifications.

Lastly, report lost credit cards or any fraud activity suspicions right away. Your bank can block your account and credit card to avoid others using it.

6. Spot unauthorized credit card charges quickly

It's essential to check your credit card statements on a regular basis. Many unauthorized charges can go unnoticed for months if you don't do this.

Review your statements early and check for any purchases that you didn't make. If you don't report it ASAP, your credit card issuer will not give you much time to dispute. Also, you might end up being liable for the charges.

Call your issuer immediately once you spot an unauthorized charge on your account.

Once your credit score is tainted with a bad record, it's difficult to fix it. You may need to endure a negative credit score for some time before you can recover from it. Protect your personal information and educate yourself of the new scams criminals develop. Always remember that these criminals will never stop finding ways to get what they want.

We don't live in a perfect, crime-free world. You must be vigilant at all times to protect your interests. You don't have to fall victim to identity theft.

Did You Know?

Some banks offer secured credit cards to people with a poor credit history or no credit history at all. Secured cards can be the best option for your first credit card. The card is "secured" with a cash balance, a savings account, for example. You cannot touch this balance, or the card will be deactivated (turned off). If you charge over your limit, the bank can take the balance from your account. Your account acts like collateral for a loan. These cards may charge higher interest rates, but they offer the convenience of using a credit card while you build a good credit history.

Chapter 13

Do-It-Yourself Credit Repair Strategies

Bad credit can be such a bane to your finances, and any other related opportunities for that matter. A low score can prevent or hinder you from enjoying certain conveniences like being approved for loans or credit cards. You'll surely be exposed to higher borrowing rates as well.

Remember that your credit score is evaluated based on your financial information through the years. Creditors will take a look at your spending habits, especially those done on credit, and take note of how often you've borrowed money and what you spent it on. They will also take a look at your repayment history.

There are plenty of factors that go into your credit score. But don't fret because there are ways by which you can repair bad credit. There are easy-to-do strategies that you can consider to improve your score and open more opportunities in the financial market.

Now these strategies will be useful but they will take time, effort, and energy. But down the line, and provided that you do things right and maintain your new score, you can enjoy peace of mind and a ton of savings for your trouble.

Here are some of the simplest ones that you can do by yourself.

1. Get a copy of your credit reports for analysis and update your personal information.

One of the simplest ways to repair your credit is by updating your personal information. The funny thing about this is that it's so simple that a limited few recognize it as a viable strategy to solve this financial conundrum.

You might be wondering how outdated personal information can affect your credit score. Well, financial institutions use your records to determine your viability for loans and similar services. By constantly updating your personal information, you'll be giving them a clearer picture as to what your situation is in terms of work and finances.

Even if you update your information, your old details won't be erased or ignored whenever your line of credit is assessed. But any improvements in your professional and financial status will work wonders for your credit health.

It's important that you update your details and make sure that you monitor all of your credit information. Apart from seeing to it that all details possessed by your creditors are correct, doing so will also help prevent the onset of fraud and identity theft.

Remember that your name, job history, or addresses won't really be factored into how your credit is scored. But there are specific personal details that will be. These details will be extremely helpful especially if you decide to dispute your credit score.

When you update your information, you'll be able to remove any negative items, if any, that may be associated with old personal details. As these negative connotations are eliminated, you can expect your credit score to rise. But don't expect the process to be a quick one. When it comes to credit repair, patience is indeed going to be a virtue.

So how can you update your personal information? For starters, you can call your local credit bureau or find them online. Depending on the available service in your area, you might be able to do everything over the phone or computer. There are times when you might have to fax over some documents to start the process.

Surely you'll be working with multiple creditors for this so make sure that you provide the same information for all of the accounts that you'll be updating. Also remember to use the same format especially when it comes to names and titles. Be prepared as there are creditors that will require you to provide the necessary paperwork as proof of legitimacy before any changes are made to your accounts.

Keep in mind that you can request for your account information and current credit reports. Simply ask your creditors for these information. Review them and see where they may be any errors, typographical and the like. Take a look at addresses, employers, aliases, maiden names, telephone numbers, emails, and other details.

If you do spot any errors or see details that need to be updated, draft a letter requesting your specific changes. Double-check the information that you provide to ensure that there won't be any further mistakes. It will take the creditors several days to process your request so monitor them and follow-up whenever necessary.

2. Consider sending dispute letters to the appropriate agencies.

There are ways to get ahold of your credit report. Chapter 2 discussed this in great detail. Your credit report will include personal details and notable transactions from which your score is based. And it's not uncommon for people to discover errors in their respective reports; errors that serve to justify ratings that are less than desirable.

Once you get a hold of your credit report, take the time to review it line by line. See if there are mismatches in the information. See if there are typographical errors. Check everything so that you know with certainty that all the available information is correct.

If you find something questionable, or if you feel as if your credit score isn't justified, then give your creditors a call. You can also send them an email indicating your concerns. It will be good if you can fix everything here. But if not, do consider sending dispute letters to the concerned parties.

In this case, a dispute letter will serve to inform the creditor of any errors you've spotted in your report. You must indicate every one of them and provide the necessary correction. So make it a point to check what you've typed so that no further errors will be recorded.

You can then include a statement as to why you feel that your credit score should be reassessed or evaluated. If you've been paying debts off on-time and haven't missed payments then you should include things like these in your request.

The objective here is to make a strong case. So the more details and proofs you can provide, the better the potential outcome may be. And always remember to be polite. Have the proper attitude and your creditors will be more than willing to help you out. You can also see a guide on how to file a dispute with the credit bureau on Chapter 2.

3. Try your best to decrease your credit utilization.

If you take a closer look at your spending habits, can you identify where exactly you use the most amount of credit? Are you someone who borrows money for large purchases, say appliances, automotive needs, or for house payments? Or are you the kind of person who needs lines of credit for everyday expenses like shopping, utility bills, and the like?

There are some people who have bad credit scores because they overuse their credit cards or borrow money when they don't need the funds. If you realize that the same situation is applicable to you then it might be a good idea to minimize your use of your existing lines of credit.

What you should understand about credit scores is that they are not affected as much by how much you borrow on occasion but how well you repay these debts. Even if you borrow less and less money per month but pay on time and in full, if possible, then you can expect your credit score to improve.

In this case, take note of how much you regularly spend in any given month. This should cover your cash expenses, credit card charges, and existing loan payments. Then see where you can cut back on your credit utilization but give yourself enough time to adjust. Start with the small things. For example, try to use cash for groceries and utility bills. Do the same for when you do your shopping.

One of the best things about cash is that you can better manage your spending when you use it. Most of the time, people tend to overspend because they don't realize how much they're spending when a card is swiped at the register. Most of the time, they end up spending more than they can afford resulting to unpaid debts at the end of the month and a decline in their credit score.

Actually, if you can go all cash for your expenses then do it. Use your lines of credit for emergency purposes only or for larger purchases. For example, have a reserve credit card for unforeseen expenses. You can also have it on hand for the occasion when your cash on hand isn't enough for an important purchase. But be disciplined enough to use it for emergency purposes only.

Reserve your lines of credit for larger requirements. For example, use your lines of credit for home and automotive loans. Use the installment function of your credit card if you were to replace some appliances at home. You can also use it for medical expenses. But make sure that if you do, your monthly income is enough for you to meet your repayment requirements.

If you were to go this route, take enough time to help yourself adjust to the significant changes. Also have a positive and persistent attitude about it moving forward. Here is where personal discipline can have the most effect on the outcome that will come your way. Always think of the bright side – this can help you improve your credit score moving forward.

4. Add other lines of credit to your portfolio.

There are times when you may have the funds but not enough access to lines of credit. In this case, it will be a good idea for you to explore the idea of adding additional credit sources to your portfolio. As mentioned previously, credit scoring depends on your credit activity. So if you don't have enough of them in your history then you can expect a less-than-average mark on your record.

There are people who have gotten so used to using cash for various transactions that they end up missing out on a number of credit-related benefits. Even if they have the money, some of them find themselves in situations where borrowing, when needed, becomes more challenging than it has to be.

Keep in mind that even if you feel that you do not need a credit card, for example, it will be a good idea to have one or several in your possession. Even if you just use them sparingly, having these transactions can help improve your credit score over time.

But apart from credit cards, also consider taking advantage of larger borrowing opportunities if you have purchases that require such. For example, if you were in the market for a new car or home, even if you have enough cash on hand, getting a loan for these can be a good way to repair your credit score.

You might be wondering why you should consider spending on interest payments if you have cash for whatever it is you'll be buying. Well, for starters, there's such a thing as inflation. So the value of your cash now will be worth less as time passes. You will be at an advantage if you resorted to monthly payments instead of paying everything up front.

Next, by not utilizing most of your cash reserves, you're putting yourself in a situation where you are as liquid as possible. Surely there will be other more urgent spending requirements that will call for cash. When these arise, you can be sure that you have the necessary resources available and ready.

Thirdly, you need to have some form of borrowing history, both long and short-term, to have a basis for financial institutions to assess your credibility. They will look at your activity, repayment, and other factors as they determine your score. You want to have a good credit rating but without any substantial borrowing, it'll be quite difficult for financial institutions to come up with this figure.

So, take a look at your portfolio. Check out your existing lines of credit and, based on your spending needs, assess what other types of credit may be of use in the future. Do understand that you won't have to engage in a transaction to have additional lines of credit added to your account.

Simply call your preferred creditor and ask that you be granted an open line should you require it in the future. Surely, they'll be happy to oblige as this will mean that you'll have a larger propensity to use their service in the future.

6. Negotiate to have your credit limits increased.

When it comes to your line of credit, it's common to have multiple creditors offering different limits per account. Some institutions may offer you just the right amount to supplement your monthly needs while others may provide you with the kind of credit limit that can allow you to make large purchases month in and month out.

It would be an excellent idea if you reviewed your credit limits. This applies to all lines of credit from credit cards to loan provisions. Call your creditors and jot down the details. Having an idea of these figures will help you make better decisions when you borrow money moving forward.

There are different issues that borrowers commonly experience; one of them being mismanaged accounts. In this case, a borrower may tend to have multiple debts or loans that they lose track of month on month.

As a result, even if they have the funds, they miss timely payments and so on and so forth. Apart from added fees, their credit scores are affected by the regular onset of late payments.

One of the best ways to prevent this issue moving forward is by trying to see if you can get your creditors to increase your lines of credit. It's not just about having an ability to borrow more money but having the ability to just borrow from one or two creditors at a time.

By compressing your borrowing activities to one or two creditors, you can prevent missed or late payments as it will be easier to track your monthly obligations. As you're able to make the right payments on time, this will positively affect your credit score. It will also reduce the need to pay finance charges and late fees on your loans.

But there's another reason why you should work towards having your lines of credit increased. Having ready access to a more sizeable amount of funds can also mean that you will have more opportunities to run these credit lines.

For a lot of people, one of the reasons why they can't easily work towards repairing their credit scores is that they're not given as many opportunities to borrow money and therefore improve their credit histories. Basically, they're stuck with poor records as they can't show their creditors that they have developed the capacity and discipline required to be considered as good borrowers.

So if you find yourself in similar situations, it might be a good idea to call your creditors and have your accounts assessed for an increase in your credit limits. You can usually call it in or send a letter of request and then it will take the financial institution a few days to come up with an answer. Note that this can cause a small reduction in your credit score but its perks in credit utilization will allow you to recover those points and get even higher scores.

Some of them might ask you for additional paperwork for them to know more about your source of funds and monthly income. Don't hesitate to provide them with the necessary details as these can also be used to update your borrower's profile.

If there's something that you should be mindful of, it is that an increased credit limit doesn't mean that you have the luxury of spending even more money on loan. It doesn't give you that luxury. Always remember to still stick with a monthly budget.

7. Work on your monthly payment schedule.

Credit revolves around one main concept and that is borrowing money regardless of the purpose. And with borrowing comes the obligation of repayment. In this case, you should set your eyes on prompt repayment.

When you borrow money, you have to make sure that you pay the agreed-upon installments on time. Not only is this essential to keep your credit score at an ideal level but it will also help you keep interest charges at a minimum. Especially if you're in a situation where you can pay-off your debt in full, what reason is there for you not to?

Before you apply for any type of loan, be it a long or short-term debt, make sure that you're fully aware of the fine print. Read the details of the loan agreement so that you won't get any nasty surprises with regards to any charges later on.

Also, make it a point to ask as many questions as possible especially when it comes to the allowable payment terms. Depending on the amount that you plan on borrowing, you may be allowed a term of anywhere from three months to five years on average for a basic loan. And different credit institutions charge varying interest fees so shop around to find the best deal with the least amount of interest payable on the debt.

Before you sign anything, make sure that the monthly payable is something that you can live with. Depending on your financial situation and monthly expenses, you want an amount that's workable; one that you won't have a difficult time paying in full.

Include your monthly debt payables when you create your monthly budget. Make sure to set aside the money for payment as soon as you get it so that you won't end up using the funds on other things. Also jot down payment due dates. Especially if you have multiple debts that need to be paid, mark your calendar or set remainders on your phone or laptop so that you won't forget about any of them.

In this case, a good discipline will be to pay the debt days before the due date. If you find due dates that fall within the same range then do consider clustering them together. This way, you can do one or two bank runs in a month and have everything paid for on time.

This cannot be stressed enough but, as much as possible, pay on time and in full. When you pay on time, you eliminate additional finance charges and penalties from being added to your account. The same goes when you pay in full. Apart from these, you also enjoy the benefits of maintaining an excellent record with your creditors, which will then be reflected on your overall credit report.

As an added benefit, paying loans in full may even qualify you for better deals in terms of lower interest charges, waived annual fees on credit cards, and other perks. So try your best to practice a little bit of discipline and plan your monthly obligations out as best as you can.

You can do something as simple as updating your profile or requesting an increase in your credit limit. Or you can choose to go with something more complex and rework your spending and repayment strategies altogether. Whatever path you choose, know that either will lead to something beneficial – a potential improvement in your credit score over time.

You can choose to speak with your creditors over the phone or there are times when you might have to consider going the more formal route and send over an email or fax a letter. For the latter, you might also have to prepare some personal documents to help solidify your claims so make sure that you have immediate access to your financial records.

There are plenty of benefits that can be enjoyed by those with excellent credit scores so do your best to ensure that these conveniences will be extended to you by financial institutions. Now the strategies that have been mentioned here can stand on their own or you can choose to combine them.

Did You Know?

MasterCard and VISA are a network of banks and financial institutions. American Express is its own company. Discover Card is a subsidiary of Morgan Stanley.

Chapter 14

Biggest Credit Mistakes and How to Avoid Them

For many people, a credit card is merely a convenient way to make transactions. However, few people realize that the little plastic card also has the ability to wreak havoc on their lives if not used carefully. Ultimately, misusing your credit account can destroy your credit scores and ultimately hamper your credit.

One way to prevent the damages that poorly handled credit can cause is to know about the mistakes that people commonly make and learn how to avoid them.

1. **Paying just the minimum**

    Issuers of credit cards set a minimum amount that you should pay every billing period. Some people have the wrong notion that this is a godsend because it is so small compared to the total amount. They couldn't be more wrong.

    Paying just the minimum amount on your credit card debt will not only increase the time it takes to pay off your balance, but it would also accrue more interest. In addition, your credit score would suffer because as your balance grows, your credit utilization grows as well and that has a negative effect on your credit score.

    To avoid having to pay more in the long run, try to pay the total balance every billing cycle. Don't let it accrue interest.

2. **Applying for too much credit**

    If you are on the checkout line and the cashier asked if you want to apply for a store credit card for the discount, do not accept it outright.

    You may love to have a discount on your purchases, but it is still a credit card. Remember that each time you apply for credit, an inquiry will show up on your credit report and will pull down your credit score a little. The discount you think you'll be getting might not be worth it.

    Also, be careful about opening too many credit accounts if you plan on applying for big loans, such as mortgage, car loan, and others.

3. **Failure to report a lost or stolen credit card immediately**

    The longer you take to file a report about your lost credit card, the longer the thief or the one who has gotten your card has to charge up your credit account.

    If you immediately report your missing card before any false charges are made, the sooner you'll avoid possible responsibilities you have to deal with for the said charges. The sooner you report a missing credit card, the sooner it would limit your liabilities for false charges.

4. **Ignoring Your Billing Statement**

    If you don't check your credit card's billing statement often, the more likely it is that you'll risk missing payment or paying less than you should have for it to be considered on time.

    In addition, ignoring your card's statement will cause you to miss some important announcements, such as an announcement to the changes on your credit card's terms.

Make it a habit to check your billing statement because it will often be your guide to know if there are any false activities on your account. Besides, doing so will help you keep your spending in check.

To make sure that the payments have been correctly applied to your account, or if the all the charges are accurate, always check your card's billing statement.

5. **Paying Late**

Always pay for your monthly payments on time. If you keep on forgetting about your due dates, then you should come up with a system that can remind you about them. For example, you can set up auto pay with your bank or use apps to set reminders. If the primary reason is inconvenience, then organize your bills so you could schedule the best time to pay all if not most of them.

If you keep on paying late for your monthly payments, it can cost you for up to $38 in late fees, which will also depend on the number of times you have been late for the past 6 months.

Also, falling behind your payments for more than 30 days will also affect your credit score. But if your existing payment is more than 60 days late, then your card's issuer may raise your interest rate up to the penalty rate available.

6. **Canceling Your Credit Card**

Now that you have finally paid off all your credit card bills which have been stressing you out for ages, your first impulse might be to get rid of your credit card as soon as possible, which is usually done by cutting up your card and closing your account.

But don't be too quick on doing that, as closing down your account so suddenly can actually lower your credit score. Keep in mind that the age of your accounts affects your credit scores.

Even if you have paid off your credit card, it would be much better for you if you just leave your credit account open, that is until you are 100% sure that you can offset the possible reduction in credit score by making changes that would boost it. Just keep it open and maintain low utilization.

7. **Not Knowing Your Credit Card Terms**

If you know how your credit card company handles the late payments, you'll be more likely to pay for your card's bill on time. After all, you'll know exactly how much they cost you.

Also, knowing about the terms of your credit card enables you to have more control over your credit's costs. You will also know how you should or shouldn't use your card, which would be based on how your creditor will react to your actions.

That's why it's important to review the terms of your credit card at least once or twice a year. You can find them on your issuer's website, or request it from their customer service.

8. **Loaning your credit card**

When you loan your credit card to another person, you will no longer have control over the purchases that they are about to make.

In the end, you'll still be responsible for paying all the bills, even if the person who borrowed your card doesn't pay you for the expenses.

Never ever loan your card to someone, even if it's someone you know, except if you are prepared to take responsibility to pay for the purchases that they are about to make.

9. **Maxing your card out**

Utilizing more than 30% of your card's limit can be quite dangerous for your credit score. Also, by getting close to your credit's limit, it will put you at risk for fees that are over the limit, and even the penalty interest will increase your card's charges once you exceed your credit card's limit.

Therefore, to have a manageable payment amount and healthy credit score, always maintain a good credit card balance.

10. **Letting your card get charged-off**

Acquiring a charge-off is one of the worst things that can happen to your credit card report and credit score. A charge-off will remain on your report for 7 years, and could significant affect your ability to get loans and credit cards several years in the future.

It would take about a total of 6 months of missed payments for you to be charged with a charge-off status. Before your card gets to that point, ensure your delinquent accounts are current.

11. **Sharing your credit card number with other people**

Some credit card holders sometimes share their card's number to pay for a bill. But if someone calls, emails, or have mailed you with some requests and unsolicited personal information, such as your Social Security number or credit card number, never reveal it even if the person sounds legitimate or nice. These kinds of requests are part of financial scams that mostly target seniors. These fraudsters are trying to make unauthorized use of your good name and credit or steal your money.

If you do become a victim of identity theft, immediately report it to your Federal Trade Commission and to your local police department.

12. **Getting pressured into accepting new cards**

Have you ever noticed that sometimes most of the letters in your mail are about new credit card offers? Or maybe you have encountered countless strangers who are calling you to pitch you one? Well, don't think that these are just your imagination, because they are not.

A lot of credit card companies send out millions or even billions of credit offers every year, but this doesn't mean that you have to accept all of their requests or listen to their sale pitches. You can freely choose to get out of the prescribed credit card offers and out of the credit card telemarketing lists.

You can also get out of the email and phone solicitations from the mortgages companies.

13. **Applying for credit repair recklessly**

If you have recently gone through a serious personal setback such as a foreclosure, divorce, or bankruptcy, your credit standing might be shaky or maybe even downright bad.

However, looking for a quick fix can actually put you in the hands of a con artist that specializes on tricking people i.e. charge you with hidden costs or high upfront fees for their fake services.

Also, be aware of companies or an individual that promises to "fix" your bad credit overnight. Fixing a really bad credit score won't happen overnight, it lasts for days, weeks, or maybe even a month if the process is slow.

14. Paying tax bills with a credit card

If you don't pay for a federal tax debt, the IRS will have the power to tax your assets, put a right to claim or hold your property, or seize your tax refunds. However, none of it should intimidate you into paying them with your credit card.

The reason is that if you use your credit card, you will also have to pay for an interchange fee. This may run anywhere from 2% to 4% of the amount that you are paying for.

Now, add those to the 12% to 18% interest that you have to pay to your bank if you think of adding the tax charge to your balance. A better solution to your problem would be to set up a repayment plan with the IRS and pay your tax debts over time.

15. Aiming for the "rewards"

We people have been known to use credit for all kinds of things, be it a lavish vacation or jewelry, or even cars and in some cases, expensive novelty products.

However, making large purchases on a credit card is definitely a no-no unless you are 100% sure that you can immediately pay off such large amounts in full.

Whatever benefits that you may gain, in terms of flier miles or hotel check-ins, will come with interest charges, which you'll have to pay if you don't immediately pay your balance off every month.

16. Using your credit card to withdraw cash

Using credit cards to withdraw cash could be bad because the credit card issuer is not able to monitor the spending, and thus view it as a high-risk loan and subsequently charge higher interests.

If you don't fully pay off the amount you withdrew within a month, your balance will start racking up some interests. Therefore, you can quickly lose control over your debt if not handled as soon as possible, particularly if you only pay the minimum amount monthly.

17. Ignoring Your Credit's Warning Signals

To improve your chances of getting a healthy credit rating, check your credit reports for free for at least once or twice a year from a government-mandated website. However, if you're in the process of building or rebuilding credit, that isn't just enough. Check it once a month. You may also want to sign up for credit monitoring services, among others.

Also take note of warning signs that indicate you might be in a debt trouble such as missing payments, only making minimum payments, regularly seeking for 0% card offers, a low-rate balance transfer just to afford payments, or charging without knowing how to pay for bills.

If any of the following warning signals are familiar to you, it's time you get your act together to start repairing your credit.

Did You Know?

In 1996, the U.S. Supreme Court in Smiley vs. Citibank lifted restrictions on the amount of late penalty fees a credit card company could charge. Additional deregulation has allowed very high interest rates to be charged.

Chapter 15

Start-up Funding Sources

Starting your own business does pose some of its own challenges. One of the biggest challenges you would face is amassing enough capital to fund your own business. Most starting business owners don't have that, unfortunately, which is why they look to other means of securing funding and other necessary resources.

There are multiple ways to do that and, for this chapter, we'd be looking at ten of them.

1. Bootstrapping Your Business

Basically, bootstrapping is starting a business with very little to no money. It also means you don't get help from angel investments or venture capital firms. What you do instead is plow back into your business the money you earn from your customers.

The 'bootstrap' word itself literally means getting into a situation using the resources in your possession. Generally, when you 'bootstrap', you are doing something difficult, on your own.

Don't get discouraged, though. A lot of businesses which have become successful started by bootstrapping.

Growing Your Money Through Bootstrapping

A bootstrapped business typically goes through these stages:

Seed money

You might start with your own personal savings, or perhaps a bit of financial help from family and friends. Just enough to get the business going. Some bootstrapped businesses even started as side business while their founders go to a regular day job. Then the founder somehow manages to save up enough money to grow the business.

Customer-funded money

Once you've started selling your services or products, you get in money from the customers. That money is then pumped back into the business. This keeps your business running which will also eventually fund the growth of the company. Growth in a bootstrapped business is usually slow. Initial funds are spent on operating expenses to keep the business running.

Loans and credits

Bootstrapping means you don't go out to get a big loan. Small loans may be required to fund some growth activities like hiring more people, evening out cash flow, or buying additional equipment. Credit becomes a secondary source of funds to keep the business operating and growing.

Pros and Cons of Bootstrapping

Bootstrapping has its own advantages and disadvantages. Here are some of them.

Pros

- **You answer only to yourself.** By funding your own business, you have full control. Businesses funded by VCs, accelerators, and angels are sometimes forced to give up equity and the fund sources themselves have their own particular interests, goals, and motivations which may not be aligned with yours. Bootstrapping gives you freedom wherein you can set your agenda and choose your directions.
- **You have focus.** Because there is little or no influence that can push your business into various directions, you can focus more on what your startup can do best – from bolstering the business' core competencies to coming up with flagship products.
- **You tend to innovate.** Necessity is said to be the mother of invention. And when you invest your own hard-earned money, necessity forces you to innovate. To invent and reinvent. Usually, because you have no other choice.
- **You become responsible.** When you own something, you tend to treat it with more care than if somebody else owns it. When you own 100 percent of the company, you'll be obsessed over the details of the business. This sense of ownership makes you more cautious and more practical in your decisions.

Cons

- **More need to generate revenue.** Because you used your own savings to fund your startup, it's essential to generate enough revenue to keep the business afloat. Early on, you need to have a successful profit plan that should be immediately operational. This necessity can result to growth paths that weren't in your original business plan. This can also hamper your growth.
- **Arrested development.** Because you don't usually have a large amount of money when you start up your business, developing key components that can fuel growth can be delayed. When you must invest part of the revenue on marketing, R&D, and hiring, you need to invest more time to plan else you'll bleed out money. Growth milestones may take more time achieve, and you'll just find yourself moving targets further.
- **Lack of connections.** In business, who you know can be as important as what you know. Other startup funding sources such as angels and crowdfunding can put you in the same room with people that open up potential markets and bolster valuable partnerships. This in turn gives you increased visibility. This is extremely difficult to do if you take the bootstrapping path.
- **Not enough credibility.** When you bootstrap, you are the only investor. Problem is, most customers will buy only from someone they know. Something that is easy if you have outside investors. Bootstrapping means you are the new kid on the block and people might think you're not credible. At least not yet. Credible investors give customers confidence to buy from you.

Basically, bootstrapping is the minimalist's approach to business. Minimalism is characterized by significant simplicity and sparseness. When you apply minimalism on your business, you're practicing bootstrapping. As much as possible, you avoid investing more money except when it's absolutely needed. You also need to work within your means and come up with ingenious ways to save money.

Bootstrapping might not be for everyone. It requires utmost discipline and restrain so that you don't go overboard when investing.

2. Crowdfunding

Basically, crowdfunding is a system of gaining business funds through collective efforts from individual investors, customers, family, and friends. Using this business approach, you can tap into these individuals via crowdfunding platforms and social media and leverage on their networks from wider reach and better exposure.

Crowdfunding is exactly the opposite of traditional business approach. With the latter, you need to do your business plan, prototypes, and market research. You then have to pitch the idea to large institutions or wealthy individuals to finance your project. Crowdfunding streamlines the traditional model because it gives the business owner a platform in building, showcasing, and sharing the pitch resources.

Types of Crowdfunding

There are several crowdfunding types or categories. What you choose as your crowdfunding method will depend on the service or product that you are offering as well as your development goals.

Donation-based crowdfunding

Basically, this type of crowdfunding means the contributors or investors are not expecting any financial return of their donations or investments. You can see a lot of donation-based crowdfunding activities like fundraising programs for medical bills, nonprofits, charities, and disaster relief.

Rewards-based crowdfunding

In a rewards-based crowdfunding system, the individual contributors to your business are offered a 'reward'. This reward is typically the service or product your business offers. Investors might be getting something in return for their investments, there's still no monetary or equity return so rewards-based crowdfunding is still considered a subset of donation-based crowdfunding. Indiegogo and Kickstarters are two of the more famous rewards-based crowdfunding platforms. They let business owners give incentives to their investors while avoiding extra expense or selling equity.

Equity-based crowdfunding

In an equity-based crowdfunding system, you allow contributors to become your business partners by giving them equity shares in return for their investment. As owners of your company's equity, these part-owners get a financial return or a share of the company's profits. This is given in the form of distribution or dividends.

Pros and Cons of Crowdfunding

Just like any other business approach, crowdfunding has some benefits and drawbacks.

Pros

- **It can save time and money.** Organizing a crowdfunding strategy is easy and fast. You don't need to do endless visits to private investors and banks.
- **You have access to capital.** Raising capital via crowdfunding usually takes less time that doing it by traditional means. A fundraising campaign is usually given a maximum of 90 days. This approach means constant negotiating, prospecting, and pitching is avoided which is the case when you get your funds

from financial institutions. You don't even have to give your investors ownership of the business. You can do the rewards-based method instead. Also, there are no upfront fees that need to be paid.

- **Easy to establish a customer base.** Getting the first customers is usually the hardest part of a new business. But if you do it via crowdfunding, you already have a group of people interested in your offering. Through crowdfunding, many of the investors become both customers and an extension of your sales team if they promote your business. This business method also helps you in engaging with the customers.

- **You can organize a marketing strategy.** Crowdfunding is basically promoting your business idea to others while seeking funds to start it up. Once you get the funds required by your business to get off the ground, you already have an idea on how to improve your marketing strategy.

- **Control on how you reward investors.** Once you get funding, you alone determine how you'll reward the investors. You have complete control of how much interest or equity you offer to them.

Cons

- **No business-to-business offerings.** People who invest in a crowdfunding initiative identify with the offering or see its benefits. That's why most offerings are aimed at consumers and not to business entities.

- **Not for complex projects.** Crowdfunding works best if the business is simple. This approach will not benefit technical or complex projects because it won't be easy to make the investors understanding. Remember that these investors are mostly common folk. Projects that require long R&D cycles are not attractive to most people so crowdfunding isn't the best way.

- **Not for large fund businesses.** There may be exceptions but crowdfunding works best for projects that need less than $100,000 of capital. If your business idea will need a larger funding, you need to consider other financial sources to raise your capital like banks and other financial institutions.

- **All or nothing.** There are crowdfunding platforms that will only release the funding for your project once the campaign has reached 100 percent or more of the funding goal. If it failed to achieve the target, your funds can be stuck in limbo.

- **Makes the project inflexible.** Drastic offering changes on your project is not allowed if you've already received the funding. Timeline delays can also hurt your brand and damage your reputation.

3. Angel Investors

Basically, angel investors are wealthy individuals who provide financial assistance for a startup. Often, these investors expect ownership stake in the business. These investors are typically called 'angels' and would invest $25,000 up to $500,000 to assist a business in getting started. Oftentimes, these angels are the last resort for startup businesses if they're not qualified for bank financing or too small for venture capitalists (VCs) to be interested in.

VCs usually demand a quick return of investment but angels are more focused on the passion and commitment of the business founders as well as the wider market opportunity. This doesn't mean they're fine with losing money. They're just not interested in making a quick buck like VCs.

The 'angel' term was once used for wealthy individuals who saved Broadway productions from closing by investing in them. There were also patrons who supported creative professionals through financial means so these artists can focus on their work. The angels of today are modern-day sympathetic financiers.

What Angels Expect

Angels can make the difference between a business startup's closure or growth. But first and foremost, they are still investors. This means that they don't want to just give away their money. They will want it back after some time. That's why angels look for certain factors that will likely improve the odds that they will get their investment back.

Keep these factors in mind when you're pitching in front of an angel:

- Your track record and experience in the business
- The business plan's viability
- A service or product that's significantly innovative or disruptive
- Scalability of the business
- Current revenue
- Exit strategy

Pros and Cons of Angel Investors

Investing through angels is not a silver bullet that can solve all your business woes like a miracle. You need to know the pros and cons before you decide it's an appropriate investment method to explore.

Pros

- **It's great for small and medium size businesses**. The funding range of $25,000 to $500,000 make angel investment a great fit if your business is small or medium in size.
- **Open to high risk ventures.** It's a given fact that more than half of new business ventures fail before reaching the fifth year. This makes it difficult to get financial help from financial institutions and VCs. What makes angels great is that they're willing to invest in business that big banks won't want to get involved with because of the high stakes. Angels don't invest in the business but rather they invest in the founder. They have their sights focused on long-term goals. You don't get that from traditional lenders like banks.
- **Offers essential knowledge.** Angel investors offer essential experience and knowledge on the table. They usually work directly with business owners and help it achieve success. Their valuable assistance may include providing business strategy suggestions, expertise and guidance, and setting up the founders with potential clients. It's important to know beforehand if your angel investor may be able to help you grow your business.
- **Tax relief.** Capital-gains rollover is just one of the several tax reliefs offered by the US federal government to angel investors. By funnelling process to small businesses, the angels are able to deter capital gains on investments made. This law helps angels retain the investment and at the same time limit the losses if ever the venture fails.

- **Quick funds.** Capital from financial institutions needs considerable time to be processed and provided to your business while angels can give it almost immediately. This is important because time is of the essence when you are starting up a business

Cons

- **Funds may not be enough.** Angels are usually individuals investing their own money and are willing to take risks. To keep the risk within acceptable limits, they limit the funds they provide. This makes angel investment inappropriate for ventures that need large capital like energy or technology so you may need to look elsewhere.
- **Return of investment.** On average, angel investors will require around 25% of the profit made by the business. This may be too high for some business owners who are trying to grow their companies.
- **Can be difficult to work with.** Unlike financial institutions who are concerned only with the returns, angels are more involved with the businesses they put their money in. You may not desire that degree of involvement from your investors.
- **Difficult to pitch to.** Angels usually support more than one venture at a time so they have a lot of things in their minds. This might make it difficult for you to get your vision across during the pitching process.
- **They look for experienced business owners.** If this is your first business venture, it might be difficult to get financial support from angel investors. Angels usually look for experienced business owners who are able to provide positive projections of the business' success.

Given the advantages and disadvantages of an angel investment, it may or may not fit the vision you have for your business. Weigh each one carefully before you pitch in front of an angel.

4. Venture Capital

Venture Capital is a form of financing in which a starting business owner gets from financial institutions, lending companies, and even well-off strangers who have shown interest in the growth of the potential business. However, venture capital is not just all about money. It can even come in the form of technical/ managerial expertise as well as assets for use in the business.

On the perspective of the investor, venture capital deals are quite a gamble. However, the pay-off if everything is successful is equally huge or more.

The appeal of venture capital deals to starting businesses is quite apparent. For starters, most of their owners have yet to access capital markets. Also, they lack the expertise to effectively run the business which a venture capital provider might just be able to provide for.

Of course, this is not without its trade-off. To get funding, a business owner has to offer something in return which is always in the form of equity. To put it simply, if that business began or was intended to be a sole proprietorship, it has now become a partnership.

How It Works

The process of securing a venture capital deal can be straightforward. First, you'd have to find a venture capital firm who would look at your business plan and determine that it is both feasible in the short-term and sustainable in the long-term.

To do that, they will do a thorough investigation on every pertinent document you will submit. This includes income forecasts, the business model, a copy of the business plan, a timeline of the management and operating history (if already established, of course), and planned product/service line.

Alternatively, you can look for Angel Investors. They may be more lenient than a VC firm but you can be certain that they may ask for a larger equity in return.

Once the company deems your plan to be sustainable, they will pledge an investment of capital in exchange for equity in the company. The investment may be provided immediately in lump sum or in increments, depending on the investor. Either way, you should get the funding/assets you need out of the deal in the soonest time possible.

Pros and Cons of Venture Capital

Before you decide to apply for a venture capital deal, however, there are a few considerations you have to keep in mind.

The Pros:

- **Significant Resource Boost** - When it comes to resources, not a lot of deals out there can match what a VC deal can offer. Depending on the investor, you might get a gradual yet substantial boost in your capital or one massive spike.
- **No Financial Liability to Investors** - VC firms and angel investors are basically gambling away their money. If you succeed with the business, they succeed. If you don't, they lose a portion of their already sizeable disposable income. Either way, you are not obligated to pay them back if the business does not take off.
- **Networking** - Not every perk with venture capital deals has to be expressed financially or in tangible assets. With the right investor, you can get the expertise you need to run the business more efficiently. Also, these investors bring with them their own network of contacts, thereby increasing your own network as well as your visibility in the market.

The Cons:

- **Loss of Full Control** - Since you are adding in people to your business with their own skills, expertise, and money, you are effectively relinquishing full control over the business. Now, every decision you make has to go through thorough discussion before being executed. This means that every decision that the business makes is more carefully thought of. However, this comes at the expense of speed.

- **Clashing Goals and Priorities** - Investors and firms do not necessarily share the same goals you have with the business. They may want the business to take a direction which you wouldn't agree with or push things at a pace you'd find either too fast or slow for your tastes.
- **Managerial Distraction** - Remember the proverb "too many cooks spoil the broth?" One of the risks with adding in new investors to the business is exposing it to ideas that may not work to its best interest. If management gets too distracted analyzing what works best, the day-to-day operations might be affected severely.

5. Business Incubators and Accelerators

Aside from adequate funding, a startup business can also find a lot of advantages in having the right amount of outside support. It's often said that business models can be improved to maximize profits.

With that in mind, it is actually possible to give a business the facelift it needs right after or before it would be set up. And this is where business incubator and accelerator programs come into play.

Which is Which?

It's a common mistake to lump these two services together as if they are just the same thing. However, this could not be further from the truth as incubator and accelerator programs actually provide different perks to businesses.

Business Incubators

The goal of incubators is to provide business owners with the chance to come up with a better business right from the start. Things like office spaces, facilities, access to research data, and training are all provided by incubation centers. Such programs are provided by mostly business organizations, universities, non-profit groups, and government agencies and are generally directed towards starting business owners.

Business incubators are generally designed to get businesses set up in whatever industry they want to operate in as soon as possible. In some programs, funding may even be provided so that the owner can spend it on securing key assets and facilities for the business. Incubator centers can also focus on one industry such as technology, health care, and finance.

Business Accelerators

At a glance, accelerators offer seemingly the same services as incubator programs. However, as the name implies, these programs are all about speed. They are usually targeting entrepreneurs who already have an idea for a great business but have no means to translate those ideas into actual and profitable products.

How the work is actually more similar to that of Venture Capital. Investors look at your business idea and determine if it is feasible or not. Each investor has their own standard so what might be profitable for one accelerator investor might be different from another.

However, if they do find that your idea can work, they will then provide initial funding and training to help you set up your business. In return, they will ask for equity in the business. This means that they share creative control with you on how to run the business.

The entire goal of accelerator program is to help you come up with a startup and launch your own products and services in the market. That successful launch will then be used to pitch to other venture capitalists, giving your business a potentially massive influx of capital.

Pros And Cons of Business Incubators and Accelerators

As with any support service, support services like incubators and accelerators bring with them their own set of perks and drawbacks. Here are some of them:

The Pros

- **Being Part of a Collective** - When starting up a business, it often feels like it's you against everybody else. There are even instances when well-established businesses in a local area are threatened by the shinier, modern-looking newcomer.
  Accelerators and incubators understand that starting up a business can be as isolating as it is difficult. As such, they primarily offer advice and guidance on how to set things right.
  What you have to understand that these programs offer more than just funding. The technical and managerial expertise you will get is vital in making the business competitive and sustainable.

- **Instant Recognition** - The best thing that you can describe about accelerators and incubators is that they are, basically, crash courses in business management. Over a short period of time, you will receive education on the latest business trends and the training on how to apply them.
  It also helps that some programs are quite well-known and certified in various industries which should help you secure funding. For instance, an investor might take a look at your business plan and notice that you have recently finished a course at a well-known accelerator/business program. That could speed up your applications for funding and make other investors less hesitant in doing business with you.

The Cons

- **They're Compulsory** - These programs are basically schools, which means that your attendance is more than necessary in some events. That time could have been otherwise used in more productive ventures such as improving on your business plan. Aside from being compulsory, the lessons you will attend might cover things that you as a business owner are already aware of or things that you might not find useful.

- **You'll Be Altering Your Plans, A Lot** - Although you do get connected to the network of these incubator/accelerator programs, that comes at the expense of you losing full control over the business. In most cases, the business plan/model you had before entering the program will not be the same when you leave it. However, you might consider these a small price to pay in ensuring that your business gets off the group as quickly as possible.

N/B: If you're interested in learning about 5 additional funding sources you can explore for your startup capital requirements, refer to the **Additional Funding Sources Booklet**

Conclusion

Understanding your credit is the first step to improving it. Hopefully, this book was able to help you do both. While there are now credit repair services, you may end up incurring debts to get them – so do be careful. Furthermore, getting such services will be useless if you don't understand how you landed a terrible credit situation in the first place.

You can improve your credit in many ways. As you learned from this book, it can be as simple as modifying your spending habits or correcting wrong information in your records. It could also be as difficult as paying all your debts at once and dealing with high interest rates. Don't forget to ditch the services that you thought would be helpful but turned out to be damaging to your finances and credit score.

Being mindful of your credit does a lot of wonders to your financial situation. It trains you to become a wise spender and keeps you away from personal bankruptcy. It also helps ensure that you won't incur debts that you can't handle. Above all, managing your credit will enable you to pursue the life you want.

It may take some time to see significant changes in your credit score. Nevertheless, you can feel some of its advantages as you keep on practicing good financial habits.

You'll need patience in enhancing your credit. After all, you're going to deal with different individuals and institutions in checking your records, correcting wrong information, and borrowing money.

The next step is to find and implement ways to increase your sources of income. You can do so by getting another job, setting up a business or investing. Make sure you have sources of both active and passive income. If you're interested in sources that will help you build passive income or just earn more money online, feel free to take a look at the second book in the Business and Money Series i.e. **Passive Income Ideas – 50 Ways to Make Money Online Analyzed.**

You may use a portion of your savings or credit to finance your new venture. With good credit score, you can get quick loan approval and low interest rate. Just keep in mind to pay your debts on time.

You're One-Of-A-Kind

In addition to everything, I would like to personally thank you for the dedication you've shown in reading this book to the end. That only shows that you are truly determined to create a better life for yourself.

It is a sad thing but the reality is that, once people start reading a book, they typically only read 10 percent of it before they give up or forget about it. Only 10 percent. What's terrible about this is that from this statistic, we can see that very few people actually follow through on what they commit to (at least when it comes to reading). The reason for this is harsh but understandable: most people are not willing to hold themselves accountable. People "want" and "want" all day, but very few actually have the fortitude to put in the work.

So what's my point? First, I am trying to tell you that if you're reading these words, you are a statistical anomaly (and I am grateful for you). But here's the kicker: in order to become successful as a result of this book, you are going to have to be in the .1 percent. You need to take action.

Set your goals and don't stop until you achieve them. Don't let anything or anyone try to discourage or bring you down. Just focus on those goals and keep on working and hustling towards them. That's what most successful entrepreneurs would do. Work hard, work smart, and be patient. These are the keys to achieving your goals. It doesn't matter if these are short-term or long-term goals.

I wish you the very best of luck!

The End

Thank you very much for taking the time to read this book. I tried my best to cover as much information as I could without overwhelming you. If you found it useful please let me know by leaving a review on Amazon! Your support really does make a difference and I read all the reviews personally so can I understand what my readers particularly enjoyed and then feature more of that in future books.

I also pride myself on giving my readers the best information out there, being super responsive to them and providing the best customer service. If you feel I have fallen short of this standard in any way, please kindly email me at **michael@michaelezeanaka.com** so I can get a chance to make it right to you. I wish you all the best with your business!

Book(s) By Michael Ezeanaka

Affiliate Marketing: Learn How to Make $10,000+ Each Month On Autopilot

Are you looking for an online business that you can start today? Do you feel like no matter how hard you try - you never seem to make money online? If so, this book has you covered. If you correctly implement the strategies in this book, you can make commissions of up to $10,000 (or more) per month in extra income.

- WITHOUT creating your own products
- WITHOUT any business or management experience
- WITHOUT too much start up capital or investors
- WITHOUT dealing with customers, returns, or fulfillment
- WITHOUT building websites
- WITHOUT selling anything over the phone or in person
- WITHOUT any computer skills at all
- WITHOUT leaving the comfort of your own home

In addition, because I enrolled this book in the kindle matchbook program, **Amazon will make the kindle edition available to you for FREE** after you purchase the paperback edition from Amazon.com, saving you roughly $6.99!!

Available In **Kindle**, **Paperback** and **Audio**

Passive Income Ideas: 50 Ways To Make Money Online Analyzed

How many times have you started a business only to later realise it wasn't what you expected? Would you like to go into business knowing beforehand the potential of the business and what you need to do to scale it? If so, this book can help you

In Passive Income Ideas, you'll discover

- A concise, step-by-step analysis of **50 business models** you can leverage to earn passive income (Including one that allows you to earn money watching TV!)
- Strategies that'll help you greatly simplify some of the business models (and in the process **make them more passive!**)
- What you can do to scale your earnings (regardless of which business you choose)
- Strategies you can implement to **minimize the level of competition** you face in each marketplace
- Myths that tend to hold people back from succeeding in their business (**we debunk more than 100 such myths!**)
- Well over 150 Insightful tips that'll give you an edge and help you succeed in whichever business you chose to pursue
- More than 100 frequently asked questions (**with answers**)

- 50 positive vitamins for the mind (in the form of inspirational quotes that'll keep you going during the tough times)
- A **business scorecard** that neatly summarizes, in alphabetical order, each business models score across 4 criteria i.e. simplicity, passivity, scalability and competitiveness
- ...and much much more!

What's more? Because the book is enrolled in kindle matchbook program, **Amazon will make the kindle edition available to you for FREE** after you purchase the paperback edition from Amazon.com, saving you roughly $6.99!!

Available In **Kindle**, **Paperback** and **Audio**

Work From Home: 50 Ways To Make Money Online Analyzed

This is a **2-in-1 book bundle** consisting of the below books. Amazon will make the kindle edition available to you for FREE when you purchase the print version of this bundle from Amazon.com - **saving you roughly 35%** from the price of the individual books.

- Passive Income Ideas – 50 Ways to Make Money Online Analyzed (Part I)
- Affiliate Marketing – Learn How to Make $10,000+ Each Month on Autopilot (Part 2)

Get this bundle at a 35% discount from Amazon.com

Available In **Kindle**, **Paperback** and **Audio**

Dropshipping: Discover How to Make Money Online, Build Sustainable Streams of Passive Income and Gain Financial Freedom Using The Dropshipping E-Commerce Business Model

---

How many times have you started a business only to later realise you had to spend a fortune to get the products manufactured, hold inventory and eventually ship the products to customers all over the globe?

Would you like to start your very own e-commerce business that gets right to making money without having to deal with all of these issues? If so, this book can help you

In this book, you'll discover:

- A simple, step-by-step explanation of what the dropshipping business is all about (**Chapter 1**)
- 8 reasons why you should build a dropshipping business (**Chapter 2**)
- Disadvantages of the dropshipping business model and what you need to look out for before making a decision (**Chapter 3**)

- How to start your own dropshipping business including the potential business structure to consider, how to set up a company if you're living outside the US, how much you'll need to start and sources of funding (**Chapter 4**)
- How the supply chain and fulfilment process works – illustrated with an example transaction (**Chapter 5**)
- Analysis of 3 potential sales channel for your dropshipping business - including their respective pros and cons (**Chapter 6**)
- How to do niche research and select winning products – including the tools you need and where to get them (**Chapter 7**)
- How to find reliable suppliers and manufacturers. As well as 6 things you need to look out for in fake suppliers (**Chapter 8**)
- How to manage multiple suppliers and the inventory they hold for you (**Chapter 9**)
- How to deal with security and fraud issues (**Chapter 10**)
- What you need to do to minimize chargebacks i.e. refund rates (**Chapter 11**)
- How to price accordingly especially when your supplier offers international shipment (**Chapter 12**)
- 10 beginner mistakes and how to avoid them (**Chapter 13**)
- 7 powerful strategies you can leverage to scale up your dropshipping business (**Chapter 14**)
- 15 practical tips and lessons from successful dropshippers (**Chapter 15**)

And much, much more!

Finally, because this book is enrolled in Kindle Matchbook Program, the **kindle edition of this book will be available to you for free** when you purchase the paperback version from Amazon.com.

If you're ready to take charge of your financial future, grab your copy of this book today! Start taking control of your life by learning how to create a stream of passive income that'll take care of you and your loved ones.

Available In **Kindle**, **Paperback** and **Audio**

Dropshipping and Facebook Advertising: Discover How to Make Money Online and Create Passive Income Streams With Dropshipping and Social Media Marketing

This is a **2-in-1 book bundle** consisting of the below books and split into 2 parts. Amazon will make the kindle edition available to you for FREE when you purchase the print version of this bundle from Amazon.com - **saving you roughly 25%** from the price of the individual paperbacks.

- Dropshipping – Discover How to Make Money Online, Build Sustainable Streams of Passive Income and Gain Financial Freedom Using The Dropshipping E-Commerce Business Model (Part 1)
- Facebook Advertising – Learn How to Make $10,000+ Each Month with Facebook Marketing (Part 2)

Available In **Kindle**, **Paperback** and **Audio**

Get this bundle at a 35% discount from Amazon.com

Real Estate Investing For Beginners: Earn Passive Income With Reits, Tax Lien Certificates, Lease, Residential & Commercial Real Estate

In this book, Amazon bestselling author, Michael Ezeanaka, provides a step-by-step analysis of 10 Real Estate business models that have the potential to earn you passive income. A quick overview of each business is presented and their liquidity, scalability, potential return on investment, passivity and simplicity are explored.

In this book, you'll discover:

- How to make money with Real Estate Investment Trusts – including an analysis of the impact of the economy on the income from REITs (**Chapter 1**)
- A step-by-step description of how a Real Estate Investment Groups works and how to make money with this business model (**Chapter 2**)
- How to become a limited partner and why stakeholders can influence the running of a Real Estate Limited Partnership even though they have no direct ownership control in it (**Chapter 3**)
- How to protect yourself as a general partner (**Chapter 3**)
- Why tax lien certificates are one of the most secure investments you can make and how to diversify your portfolio of tax lien certificates (**Chapter 4**)
- Strategies you can employ to earn passive income from an empty land (**Chapter 5**)
- Two critical factors that are currently boosting the industrial real estate market and how you can take advantage of them (**Chapter 6**)
- Some of the most ideal locations to set up industrial real estate properties in the US, Asia and Europe (**Chapter 6**)
- Why going for long term leases (instead of short term ones) can significantly increase you return on investment from your industrial real estate properties (**Chapter 6**)
- Why commercial properties can serve as an excellent hedge against inflation – including two ways you can make money with commercial properties (**Chapter 7**)
- How long term leases and potential 'turnover rents' can earn you significant sums of money from Retail real estate properties and why they are very sensitive to the state of the economy (**Chapter 8**)
- More than 10 zoning rights you need to be aware of when considering investing in Mixed-Use properties (**Chapter 9**)
- 100 Tips for success that will help you minimize risks and maximize returns on your real estate investments

And much, much more!

PLUS, **BONUS MATERIALS**: you can download the author's Real Estate Business Scorecard which neatly summarizes, in alphabetical order, each business model's score across those 5 criteria i.e. liquidity, scalability, potential return on investment, passivity and simplicity!

Finally, because this book is enrolled in Kindle Matchbook Program, the **kindle edition of this book will be available to you for free** when you purchase the paperback version from Amazon.com.

If you're ready to take charge of your financial future, grab your copy of This Book today!

Available In **Kindle**, **Paperback** and **Audio**

Credit Card And Credit Repair Secrets: Discover How To Repair Your Credit, Get A 700+ Credit Score, Access Business Startup Funding, And Travel For Free Using Reward Cards

Are you sick and tired of paying huge interests on loans due to poor credit scores? Are you frustrated with not knowing where or how to get the necessary capital you need to start your business? Would you like to get all these as well as discover how you can travel the world for FREE?

If so, you'll love Credit Card and Credit Repair Secrets.

Imagine knowing simple do-it-yourself strategies you can employ to repair your credit profile, protect it from identity theft, access very cheap and affordable funding for your business and travel the world without any out of pocket expense!

This can be your reality. You can learn how to do all these and more. Moreover, you may be surprised by how simple doing so is.

In this book, you'll discover:

- **3 Types of consumer credit (And How You Can Access Them!)**
- How To Read, Review and Understand Your Credit Report (Including a Sample Letter You Can Send To Dispute Any Inaccuracy In It)
- **How To Achieve a 700+ Credit Score (And What To Do If You Have No FICO Score)**
- How To Monitor Your Credit Score (Including the difference between hard and soft inquiries)
- **What The VantageScore Model Is, It's Purpose, And How It Differs From The FICO Score Model**
- The Factors That Impact Your Credit Rating. Including The Ones That Certainly Don't - Despite What People Say!
- **Which Is More Important: Payment History Or Credit Utilization? (The Answer May Surprise You)**
- Why You Should Always Check Your Credit Report (At least Once A Month!)
- **How Credit Cards Work (From The Business And Consumer Perspective)**
- Factors You Need To Consider When Choosing A Credit Card (Including How To Avoid A Finance Charge on Your Credit Card)
- **How To Climb The Credit Card Ladder And Unlock Reward Points**
- Which Is More Appropriate: A Personal or Business Credit Card? (Find Out!)
- **How to Protect Your Credit Card From Identity Theft**
- Sources of Fund You Can Leverage To Grow Your Business

And much, much more!

An Identity Theft Resource Center (ITRC) report shows that 1,579 data breaches exposed about 179 million identity records in 2017. Being a victim of an identity scam can cause you a lot of problems. One of the worst cases would be the downfall of your credit score. You don't have to fall victim to it.

This book gives you a simple, but incredibly effective, step-by-step process you can use to build, protect and leverage your stellar credit profile to enjoy a financially stress-free life! It's practical. It's actionable. And if you follow it closely, it'll deliver extraordinary results!

PLUS BONUS - because this book is enrolled in Kindle Matchbook Program, the **kindle edition of this book will be available to you for free** when you purchase the paperback version from Amazon.com.

If you're ready to take charge of your financial future, grab your copy of This Book today!

Available In **Kindle**, **Paperback** and **Audio**

Real Estate Investing And Credit Repair: Discover How To Earn Passive Income With Real Estate, Repair Your Credit, Fund Your Business, And Travel For Free Using Reward Credit Cards

This is a **2-in-1 book bundle** consisting of the below books and split into 2 parts. Amazon will make the kindle edition available to you for FREE when you purchase the print version of this bundle from Amazon.com - **saving you roughly 25%** from the price of the individual paperbacks.

- Real Estate Investing For Beginners – Earn Passive Income With Reits, Tax Lien Certificates, Lease, Residential & Commercial Real Estate (Part 1)
- Credit Card And Credit Repair Secrets – Discover How To Repair Your Credit, Get A 700+ Credit Score, Access Business Startup Funding, And Travel For Free Using Reward Cards (Part 2)

Available In **Kindle**, **Paperback** and **Audio**

Get this bundle at a 35% discount from Amazon.com

Passive Income With Dividend Investing: Your Step-By-Step Guide To Make Money In The Stock Market Using Dividend Stocks

Have you always wanted to put your money to work in the stock market and earn passive income with dividend stocks?

What would you be able to achieve with a step-by-step guide designed to help you grow your money, navigate the dangers in the stock market and minimize the chance of losing your capital?

Imagine not having to rely solely on a salary or a pension to survive. Imagine having the time, money and freedom to pursue things you're passionate about, whether it's gardening, hiking, reading, restoring a classic car or simply spending time with your loved ones.

This book can help you can create this lifestyle for yourself and your loved ones!

Amazon bestselling author, Michael Ezeanaka, takes you through a proven system that'll help you to build and grow a sustainable stream of passive dividend income. He'll show you, step by step, how to identify stocks to purchase, do accurate due diligence, analyze the impact of the economy on your portfolio and when to consider selling.

In this book, you'll discover:

- Why investing in dividend stocks can position you to benefit tremendously from the "Baby Boomer Boost" (Chapter 1)
- **Which certain industry sectors tend to have a higher dividend payout ratio and why? (Chapter 2)**
- How to time your stock purchase around ex-dividend dates so as to take advantage of discounted share prices (Chapter 2)
- **Why a stock that is showing growth beyond its sustainable rate may indicate some red flags. (Chapter 2)**
- 5 critical questions you need to ask in order to assess if a company's debt volume will affect your dividend payment (Chapter 3)
- **How high dividend yield strategy can result in low capital gain taxes (Chapter 4)**
- Reasons why the average lifespan of a company included in the S&P 500 plummeted from 67 years in the 1920s to just 15 years in 2015. (Chapter 5)
- **A blueprint for selecting good dividend paying stocks (Chapter 6)**
- The vital information you need to look out for when reading company financial statements (Chapter 7)
- **A strategy you can use to remove the emotion from investing, as well as, build wealth cost efficiently (Chapter 8)**
- An affordable way to diversify your portfolio if you have limited funds (Chapter 9)
- **Why you may want to think carefully before selling cyclical stocks with high P/E ratio (Chapter 10)**

And much, much more!

PLUS BONUS - because this book is enrolled in Kindle Matchbook Program, the **kindle edition of this book will be available to you for free** when you purchase the paperback version from Amazon.com.

Whether you're a student, corporate executive, entrepreneur, or stay-at-home parent, the tactics described in this book can set the stage for a financial transformation.

If you're ready to build and grow a steady stream of passive dividend income, Grab your copy of this book today!

Available In **Kindle**, **Paperback** and **Audio**